COME, LET US WORSHIP

A PRACTICAL GUIDE TO THE
Divine Liturgy for Orthodox Laity

V. Rev. Fr. Patrick B. O'Grady

ANCIENT FAITH PUBLISHING

CHESTERTON, INDIANA

Come, Let Us Worship: A Practical Guide to the
Divine Liturgy for Orthodox Laity
Copyright © 2016 by Patrick O'Grady

All rights reserved.

Published by:
  Ancient Faith Publishing
  A Division of Ancient Faith Ministries
  1050 Broadway, Suite 6
  Chesterton, IN 46304

ISBN: 978-1-936270-50-7

With the blessing of His Eminence,
the Most Reverend Archbishop JOSEPH,
Metropolitan of New York and All North America
Antiochian Orthodox Christian Archdiocese of North
America

Cover photo by MRD photo and used with permission

24 23 22 21 20 19   15 14 13 12 11 10 9 8 7 6 5 4 3 2

Contents

Preface 5

1: Introduction 9
What Is the Divine Liturgy? 9
Where Does the Divine Liturgy Come From? 22
When Is the Divine Liturgy Celebrated? 26

2: The Organization of the Divine Liturgy 33
The Three Basic Parts of the Liturgy 33
Entry into the Church 42

3: The Divine Liturgy in Detail 47
The Liturgy of the Word 47
The Liturgy of the Eucharist 66
Concluding Remarks 103

Appendix A:
Personal Preparation for Holy Communion 105

Appendix B:
Laymen Entering & Serving in the Holy Altar 111

Appendix C:
Standing or Sitting in Vespers and Orthros   115
   Vespers with an Entrance   *115*
   Orthros with a Gospel Reading   *116*

Glossary   119

Preface

The Church is the temple of God, the holy precinct, the house of prayer, the assembling together of the people, the body of Christ, His name, the bride of Christ, calling forth the peoples for repentance and prayer.... The Church is an earthly heaven, in which the heavenly God dwells and moves about.

ST. GERMANOS, PATRIARCH OF
CONSTANTINOPLE (EIGHTH CENTURY)

THE MOST PROFOUND ACT OF PRAYER that takes place in the Church is the Holy and Divine Liturgy. Through the Liturgy, God the Lover and man the beloved enter into a communion of love that purifies and illumines man and glorifies God. Man raises his whole person-in-community and, through his shared nature with the creation itself, all things to God in a movement of free return to the ancient Beauty through the Divine Liturgy. This is Giver and

Gift; it is a movement of eternal life, of divine energy, revealing the age to come, the Kingdom of God.

This booklet promotes a greater awareness about the meaning of the Divine Liturgy insofar as human words are capable of stating it. The author seeks a more heartfelt, intelligent, practical, and even physical engagement with the praying of the Liturgy. Through our participation with faith and knowledge in the act of liturgizing, the whole of our Orthodox way of life takes on greater meaning and leads us to the acquisition of godliness and "holiness without which no one can see the Lord."

Many years ago, a pious layman, Robert S. Andrews, wrote a guide to the Liturgy, *In Remembrance of Me,* from which this revision takes its inspiration. The title has been changed, and the booklet has been completely rewritten to meet the specific demands of a new generation of worshippers, more and more of whom grew up outside of Orthodoxy and, in some cases, outside of any meaningful Christian formation. Many converts to Orthodoxy bring concepts inherited from previous experiences that are at odds with the Holy Tradition. So the author has undertaken a revision of the whole work.

Since there are always many questions raised and since oftentimes firm and dogmatic assertions tend to be made on slender bases, special attention has been given to practical instructions as to what exactly to do at each part of the Liturgy. There is wide variation in some areas in acceptable practice across the Church; however, the directions given in this booklet from the "Mediterranean" practice will help all who read this book to be more intentional and involved in practicing their own accepted tradition, wherever it may differ. When in doubt, one should refer questions of specific devotional practices to his or her parish priest and spiritual father.

Biblical quotations are generally taken from the *Orthodox Study Bible* (OSB, Thomas Nelson, 2008). At times, I offer my own translation; these cases are carefully noted. Citations from the Psalms are taken from *The Psalter of the Seventy* (Holy Transfiguration Monastery, 1974), and the traditional Orthodox enumeration of the Psalter is employed (LXX=Septuagint). If the reader uses a non-Orthodox Bible to look up the references to the Psalms, he will need to make a conversion, as follows:

✤ Psalms 1–8 and 148–150 bear the same enumeration for both LXX and Western Bibles.

✤ Psalm 9 (LXX) = Psalms 9 and 10 (Western)

✙ Psalms 10–112 and 116–145 (LXX) = same number + 1 (Western). *E.g., Ps 50 (LXX) = Ps 51 (Western)*

✙ Psalm 113 (LXX) = Psalms 114 and 115 (Western)

✙ Psalms 114 and 115 (LXX) = Psalm 116 (Western)

✙ Psalms 146 and 147 (LXX) = Psalm 147 (Western)

Heartfelt gratitude is expressed to the Most Reverend Metropolitan Joseph of the Antiochian Orthodox Christian Archdiocese of North America for his blessing and promotion of the publication of this booklet.

Mr. Andrews, the author of the original guide to the Liturgy that inspired this revision, stated in his preface, "This work is presented in humility, with the hope that it adds to the knowledge of Orthodoxy and the Church of Jesus Christ." I say my "Amen" to this hope.

THE ARCHPRIEST PATRICK B. O'GRADY

Introduction

What Is the Divine Liturgy?

Stand fast and hold the traditions which you were taught.

2 THESS. 2:15

The Divine Liturgy is the highest form of prayer in which a sacred exchange takes place. Mankind offers to God "his temporal and limited life [in exchange] for the eternal and infinite life of God."

ELDER ZACHARIAS OF ESSEX

The Divine Liturgy is God's offering to man, and man's offering to God.

HIEROMONK GRIGORIOS OF KOUTLOUMOUSIOU

The Divine Liturgy is the sacred work of the entire Church, the clergy with the people. . . . All [the ranks of the clergy, monastics, and lay persons] work together in the ritual action of divine worship and all reap the fruits of spiritual goods and the gifts of the Holy Spirit, all of which flow forth from this ritual.

IOANNIS FOUNTOULIS

THE COMMON PRAYER OF CHRISTIANS

CHRISTIANS HAVE ALWAYS gathered together on the first day of the week, and at other special times, to offer their prayers in common and to bring gifts of bread and wine, according to the commandment of our Lord God and Savior Jesus Christ. The Liturgy is the holy tradition of worship, the "sacrifice of praise," that accomplishes these things.

When an Orthodox Christian places his first priority on the remembrance of God, he begins the new week by attending the service of Vespers on the evening before the first day of the week, keeps a holy silence in his heart until the Liturgy "on the morning of the Day of the Sun," and defers all other obligations in his life until after accomplishing the mystical sacrifice. By putting God first, he finds meaning in all his labors in the new week now unfolding before him. As the holy Apostle James teaches us, "If any of you lacks wisdom, let him ask of God, who gives to all liberally" (James 1:5). Every one of us needs wis-

Introduction

dom to face the myriad problems that present themselves to us every day: personal, familial, work- or school-related. If God comes first, then we can meet every problem with confidence, knowing that His merciful grace will guide us toward what is pleasing to Him and good for our salvation.

Why must we pray at church? Why not pray alone, in our homes, or in the woodlands, or in any beautiful place indoors or out? Why must a person pray at a certain place? Does not the Bible say that "God does not live in houses made by man"? These questions are constantly posed by many in our times. And, to tell the truth, the answer is simply that we may pray to God in any place, at any time, and under any circumstances.

However, God has always summoned man to pray to Him and to offer Him due worship at specific times and in specific places for specific purposes. Not all prayer is of the same depth—or height. That great liturgist and ecumenical father, St. John Chrysostom, taught us, "If we pray alone, our prayer is weak and ineffectual. But when we pray in church with the community in the Liturgy, our prayer becomes very powerful." Our Lord Jesus taught us, "For where two or three are gathered together in My name, I am there in the midst of them" (Matt. 18:20). The priest cites these very words in the prayer of the third antiphon said just before the Little Entrance, the first solemn act of the Divine Liturgy.

Under this heading, a comment can be made regarding timeliness in showing up for the Liturgy. It is best to arrive for or during the service that precedes the Liturgy (Orthros, or in some traditions, the Hours). It is also fine to arrive during the enarxis of the Liturgy itself (the opening portion, up until the Entrance with the Gospel). If you arrive after the Entrance, you are late; and if you arrive after the reading of the Holy Gospel, you should refrain from receiving Holy Communion (unless you have a pastoral exception from your priest that explicitly allows for this, due to some personal exigency).

BETTER EXPERIENCED THAN UNDERSTOOD

Above all, the Liturgy is known through experience. Jesus said to His first followers, in response to their inquiry, "Come and see!" Our Lord did not engage them in a theological dispute or a long-winded talk; rather, He invited them to experience Him, the Author of Life. However, St. Peter, one of Christ's first disciples, admonished us to build upon our experience: "Add to your faith virtue, to virtue knowledge" (2 Peter 1:5). So it helps a great deal if

Introduction

we participate in the Liturgy with some knowledge of what is going on. This little book gives the reader basic information about the Liturgy as an aid in participating in it with deeper awareness.

Ask the Lord and your spiritual father to help you to put into practice the holy things taught here and to be obedient to these exhortations. Wherever things stated here differ in some small way from what you have learned from your priest, discuss it with him, and out of respect for him, always defer in love to his specific direction. If you do these things in humility and love, you will find the peace that passes understanding (see Phil. 4:7) in all that you do. Your active participation in the Liturgy will energize your faith.

UNIQUE VOCABULARY ABOUT THE LITURGY

As with any field of human endeavor, specialized vocabulary describes the elements of that field. The worship of God is no different. Many of the most basic words of the Bible are frequently used in the Liturgy, in their original biblical language, so filled with meaning that they cannot be translated easily: *amen, alleluia, kyrie eleison, eucharist, Theotokos, Christ, trisagion,* and many more. A glossary of this special liturgical vocabulary is provided at the end of this book for the reader's handy reference. The glossary explains these words in simple terms as an aid in reading this book and in understanding the richness of the Divine Liturgy.

THE BODILY MOVEMENTS OF PRAYER IN THE LITURGY

Before we begin our commentary, we must say something about how to participate bodily in the Liturgy. Orthodox Christian faith is deeply incarnational; that is, the whole person is involved with prayer. "You shall love the LORD your God with all your heart, with all your soul, with all your mind, and with all your strength. . . . You shall love your neighbor as yourself" (Mark 12:30–31). Many things can be said of this profound teaching of our Lord Jesus Christ. However, in this paragraph, we restrict ourselves to looking only at the truth that the whole person worships, not just the mind. In the commentary below, at the head of each section, the appropriate bodily posture and bodily action for that part of the Liturgy will be noted. These actions include the following:

Standing

We stand erect, not leaning against anything, hands at the side, over the heart, or modestly upraised (any of these positions, without drawing others' attention to ourselves). Standing is the default posture unless noted otherwise. "Praise the Lord, ye who stand in the house of the Lord" (Ps. 133:1–2).

Bowing, metania

There are two kinds of *metanias*, a great metania to the ground (prostration) and a little metania (bow from the waist only). The first is not used in the Divine Liturgy, since it implies penitential reverence—a spiritual ethos not appropriate to the festal and paschal character of any Divine Liturgy, whether held on Sunday or a weekday. However, the little metania (a bow from the waist, with right hand extended, palm facing outward, to the floor, and arising again to the upright position) is used several times in the Liturgy at the places so designated in this commentary.

The sign of the cross ("making a cross")

The act of signing oneself with the Cross is a profound act of prayer. "The light of Thy countenance hath been signed upon us" (Ps. 4:7).

"This sign, according to oldest custom, we make in the following manner: the thumb, the index and the middle fingers of the right hand we join together (representing the three hypostases of the Holy Trinity, Father, Son, and Holy Spirit), while we bend down the third and the little fingers till they touch the palm of the hand (representing the divine and human natures of Christ in hypostatic union). Having disposed the fingers after this fashion, we touch with them first, the brow, then the breast (i.e., where chest meets abdomen), and after that, first the right shoulder and then the left, thus making on our persons the sign of the cross" (Fr. Basil Kherbawi, 1931).

There are many indications for the sign of the cross in the Liturgy, as given in detail below. It is always fitting to sign yourself with the cross as you are inspired through humble prayer, as long as you observe modesty and do not disturb those around you.

We may sign ourselves with the cross:[1]

✠ whenever we pass the center line (east-west axis) of the nave, thus passing the Holy Table

✠ before venerating an icon, the cross, or the Gospel

✠ at the opening exclamation of the Liturgy, "Blessed is the kingdom"

✠ whenever the priest says "glory" in the exclamation at the end of any priestly prayer (as this

---

[1] These practices vary among different traditions. Follow the practice of your parish.

Introduction

anticipates the utterance of the name of the Holy Trinity)

✟ at the beginning and end of the Gospel reading

✟ during the Creed, upon hearing the words "(the Holy Spirit) . . . who with the Father and the Son is worshipped and glorified"

✟ in the Anaphora, at the words "Thine own of Thine own"

✟ before approaching the chalice (and followed by the folding of the arms crosswise), in order to commune in the Holy Mysteries

✟ after the Liturgy, before taking antidoron (blessed bread)

However, we do not make the sign of the cross:

✟ when the bishop or priest blesses us with the Peace

✟ when the priest or deacon honors us with incense (because we are being blessed)

✟ when we are directly in front of the chalice to commune, so as not to risk upsetting the chalice in the priest's hands

✠ outside of the services, when we take a personal blessing from the bishop or priest (because we are *being* "signed")

Inclining the head
The inclination (bowing) of the head is appropriate whenever the priest blesses the people with the Peace, whenever the priest or deacon censes toward the people, and at the Prayer of Inclination, which follows the Lord's Prayer at the diaconal prompt, "Bow your heads unto the Lord!"

Hands over the heart
That is, the placement of the right hand over the heart and the left hand over the right hand. This posture can express intense humility and may be observed at several moments in the Liturgy, especially during the recitation of the tenth pre-Communion Prayer, "I believe, O Lord, and I confess . . ." We assume this posture during our approach to and reception of Holy Communion (see Appendix A).

Lifting of the hands
The lifting of the hands, with palms facing upward, is much mentioned in the Holy Scriptures as a posture

for prayer; for example, "Lift up your hands unto the Lord, O ye servants of the Lord" (Ps. 133:2; see also Ps. 62:4). The Church has learned in her long experience to teach the faithful to be modest in this posture, as it can easily cause disorder in the liturgical community. Indeed, the excessive raising of hands is a hallmark of heterodox enthusiastic and Pentecostal groups. Holy counsel teaches us not to raise the hands above the level of our eyes and ears, at the highest, and to maintain this posture only for brief periods of time in public prayer.

Veneration (kissing) of icons

We venerate the icons by kissing them lightly with the lips. Some also touch the icon with the forehead after kissing it.[2] The public act of venerating the icon is a hallmark of Orthodoxy, mentioned expressly in the hymnody on the Sunday of the Triumph of Orthodoxy (first Sunday of Lent). Let us never be ashamed to perform this profound act of worship.

Be sure your lips are free of any lipstick or makeup. It is always poor manners and even harmful to certain icons to leave lip marks. Approach the icon on the *proskynetarion* (icon stand). Make two metanias

---

[2] In the Russian tradition, this is done only when a relic is present.

with the sign of the cross in front of the icon. Then kiss the right foot or right hand (or, lacking them depicted, the right shoulder) of the central figure in the icon. Never venerate the face directly. Light your candle(s), as you wish, then make one more metania and cross and move aside to your place.

Lighting candles
The act of lighting a candle is a beautiful form of embodied prayer that shows the light of Christ present for our own and others' salvation. Christ is "the Light of the world"; lighting a candle expresses this truth in combination with our prayer for our family members and others, as we feel moved to pray. Take your tapers as you enter the narthex, and leave your monetary offering in support of the parish to pay for the tapers. Approach to venerate the icon, then light and place your taper(s) in the place designated and take your place in the assembly. Wait to light your taper if some liturgical action is taking place, so as not to cause a distraction to others.

Using the voice to sing or to recite
We use our voice in singing the hymns (according to your local parish tradition) and prayerful responses, such as "Lord, have mercy," "To Thee, O Lord,"

and others to be mentioned below, and especially in saying the Creed, the Lord's Prayer, and the (tenth) Pre-Communion Prayer, "I believe, O Lord, and I confess..."

Sitting (always attentively; never casually)
There is no indication for sitting as a posture of prayer, strictly speaking. However, for practical reasons, parish churches usually provide some seating (either throughout the church or around the perimeter). When sitting in church, we avoid a casual attitude. That is, we do not cross our legs or assume any leisurely posture. Both feet should always be in contact with the floor, so that we are ready to stand at the diaconal prompt, "Let us attend!" or "Stand aright!"

There are two places in the Liturgy when sitting is precisely indicated, although never required:

✠ during the reading of the Apostle[3]

✠ during the delivery of the homily.

Out of respect for the presence of the Holy Gifts during the distribution of Holy Communion, standing through this period of the Liturgy constitutes good liturgical manners and is encouraged. Obviously,

---

3 In the Russian tradition, only the clergy sit during the Apostle; the people stand.

in cases of weakness, sickness, old age, and the like, sitting may be necessary. If in doubt, discuss this with your priest or sponsor.

Where Does the Divine Liturgy Come From?

THE CULMINATION OF THE AGE-OLD TRADITION OF WORSHIP

> *Thy processionals have been seen, O God, the processionals of my God, of my King Who is in His sanctuary. Princes went before, and after them the chanters, in the midst of timbrel-playing maidens. In the congregations bless ye God, the Lord from the well-springs of Israel. (Ps. 67:25–27)*

Immediately after the exile of our common ancestors, Adam and Eve, from the Eden of delight, men built altars and prayed to God, accompanied by sacrifices of various kinds. Noah built an altar after the great Deluge, as did Abraham and the patriarchs, our forefathers who received the first promises from God. Moses was instructed to build a specific tent of worship, the Tabernacle in the wilderness. Later, King David's son, Solomon, received the command to build God a house of worship, the first temple in Jerusalem. All this was to teach man that liturgical worship,

Introduction

under the direction of the ministers duly appointed by God, comprises the highest form of prayer—the pinnacle of spiritual experience: *I was glad because of them that said unto me: Let us go into the house of the Lord* (Ps. 121:1).

The Holy and Divine Liturgy is the product of two elements. First, our Liturgy is founded on the order of worship taught by God to Moses in the Old Testament. Later, under the ministry of Ezra the prophet (sixth century BC), the interpretation of Scripture was added to Mosaic tradition. Then finally, the Mystical Supper itself, the direct instruction given by Our Lord Jesus Christ on the eve of His Passion, was incorporated to complete the Holy and Divine Liturgy. On that night, He gave Himself to us mystically in the offered bread, His Body, and in the wine, His Blood.

After Christ's glorious Resurrection "on the third day" (Sunday), He appeared many times to His Apostles and taught them "the things pertaining to the kingdom of God" (Acts 1:3). The Church has always understood this to mean, among other things, direct instruction to them concerning the Liturgy. In the Book of Acts, we learn about the sending forth of St. Paul on his apostolic journeys. He went out from Antioch, where the Church, inspired by the Holy

Spirit, laid hands on him to commission him for that work. The text literally says "while they were *celebrating the Liturgy* [Greek *leitourgountes,* "liturgizing"] unto the Lord, and praying and fasting" (Acts 13:2, 3). So the Liturgy is the fundamental and most profound way in which the Church shows herself to be what she is: the New Israel, the Bride and Body of Christ.

PRODUCT OF DIVINE REVELATION AND GREAT HUMAN CULTURAL ACHIEVEMENT

The Divine Liturgy comes to us from the Lord Himself and is celebrated by His apostles and their successors, the Orthodox Catholic bishops, right down to our time, in an uninterrupted, continuous expression of faith and love. This living process will continue, without a doubt, by God's holy Providence, until the Lord Himself appears again to "judge the living and the dead."

St. Paul informs us, in his First Epistle to the Corinthians, that he "received from the Lord" (11:23) that which he passed on to the Corinthians—namely, the Eucharist, in which bread and wine are offered. The bread becomes the Body of Christ; and the wine, the Blood of Christ. This practice of liturgizing was spread by all of the Apostles throughout the ancient world. After their passing from this transitory life to their reward, the Liturgy was celebrated in every place with both exacting uniformity and marvelous diversity. The uniformity is expressed in the central act of calling down the Holy Spirit, a little Pentecost, in which Christ becomes present to the faithful. This is the divine nature of the Liturgy: changeless, mystical, transcendent, surpassing the understanding, a pure prayer.

The diversity of the Liturgy is expressed by the development of localized and distinctive ways of performing the Liturgy. These various local ways of celebrating the Eucharist can be classified into liturgical families, just as human beings can cite their own personal and familial genealogies. For example, the Liturgy was celebrated in a certain precise way in Jerusalem and in Antioch, and in another way in Rome, and still another way in Alexandria, and so on. The Antiochene way of liturgizing was carried by St. John Chrysostom (in the fourth century) to New Rome (Constantinople), where it became the basis for the Constantinopolitan, or imperial, "Great Church" Liturgy. This was somewhat different from the way the Liturgy was prayed in Alexandria; and as I said, yet different again in the West—in old Rome, Lyons (Gaul), and Milan. This diversity expresses the human nature of the Liturgy. Like Jesus our

Lord Himself, who possesses two natures "inseparable yet unconfused," so the Liturgy possesses both a divine, changeless aspect as well as a human, linguistic, and cultural expression, which is subject to constant change over the centuries and from one place to another.

When Is the Divine Liturgy Celebrated and by Whom?

The Liturgy may be served on any day, throughout the year, with an important exception. During the weekdays of the week before Lent and Great Lent itself, and on Monday, Tuesday, Wednesday, and Friday of Holy Week, no Liturgy with the consecration of bread and wine may be celebrated. So we do not serve the Anaphora during Holy Week, except for Holy Thursday (the annual memorial of the Eucharist) and Holy Saturday (the Vesperal Liturgy of Pascha).

Instead, on appointed days in Lent, we serve a special form of the Liturgy, called the Liturgy of the Presanctified Gifts. This special Liturgy is celebrated without the Anaphora and is actually a very compunctionate service of Holy Communion. That is why it is called "Presanctified": the bread and wine presented here were consecrated on the previous Sunday. Also, during Lent, the usual form of the Liturgy, that of St. John Chrysostom, is served only on Saturday, but the older and longer form of the Liturgy, that of St. Basil, is served on Sundays.

Although other forms of the Liturgy are served periodically at certain times of the year, the most common form of the Divine Liturgy celebrated in the Orthodox Catholic Church throughout the world is that of St. John Chrysostom, a pastorally beautiful Liturgy in which Chrysostom abbreviated the longer prayers inherited from the ancient Jerusalemite Liturgy of St. James and the profoundly theological Liturgy of St. Basil.

Before we examine the Liturgy in detail, with a view toward how best to participate in it, let us see when in the course of the day it is best to celebrate the Liturgy.

THE LITURGY IN TIME

The Liturgy is independent from the daily cycle of time. This movement of time through the day is marked in the Church by special services of worship: Vespers at sunset (the beginning of the new day), Compline after the evening meal, the Midnight service, Orthros before sunrise, and the canonical Hours (First, Third, Sixth, and Ninth) through the daylight hours. In parish churches, only Third Hour (prayed before the Liturgy if Orthros is done the night before), Vespers, and Orthros (also called Matins) are regularly celebrated, according to the parish needs, except during Great Lent and Holy Week, when services in the parish usually become more frequent and less abbreviated.

Each of the daily services of prayer marks time and sanctifies it. But the Liturgy itself transcends time and therefore does not mark time in any way. Although the Liturgy can be served at any time of day or night, usually it is served in the morning (preceded by the service of Orthros, or the service of the Hours, depending upon local tradition). Therefore, faithful Orthodox Christians make it a habit to attend Vespers (or Vigil) on the night before the Liturgy and to keep a quiet evening with prayer and preparation, as strength enables. Early in the morning, the faithful return to the church temple for Orthros (or Hours) and remain for the Liturgy. This is the context in time, as usually celebrated in the parishes of most Orthodox churches. The services of Orthros and the Hours are not in themselves a preparation for the Liturgy, strictly speaking; rather, these services have their own theological and prayerful ethos.

The Liturgy is not one service among many; it is

Introduction

in a class by itself. The faithful pray chiefly through listening in the other services; however, in the Divine Liturgy, they share in the liturgical work of prayer as a priestly community (1 Peter 2:9). This does not demean the other services; all the services function in unique ways to edify and build up the Body of Christ. The Liturgy, however, is the culmination of our worship.

The services of the daily cycle (Vespers, Orthros, Hours) assist the faithful to ascend noetically (spiritually) the "holy mountain" of the heart to converse with God liturgically. Imagine a family working together to prepare a special meal. The vegetables are washed and cut, savory meats are roasted, the wine is chilled, the table is set, desserts are set out. Perhaps an appetizer tray is made ready. The family converses, maybe sings as they work. All have a part to play; all contribute. Finally all is ready. The family gathers around the table as the father gives the blessing, and all sit down to share the meal.

We have seen that the Liturgy is, basically, a sacred meal. This meal needs preparation. So you can see how unprepared and ill-fitted each of us might be if we showed up late merely to "get Communion." We are not really present with full attentiveness; our heart and mind are still distracted by worldly cares.

We have not been involved in the work of preparation. So try to observe the services on the eve of the Liturgy and come to church early to hear Orthros or the Hours before the Liturgy begins. Then your heart is warmed and your mind is attentive to the presence of the Lord. You have fully participated in the sacred work of prayer.

WHAT "LITURGY" IS AND WHO THE PARTICIPANTS ARE

In the original Greek, the word *liturgy* is actually made of two elements (*leitos*, "people," and *ergeia*, "working"), the oldest and primary meaning of which is "the work of the people," or "a public service." In pre-Christian antiquity, this word meant the "duty" or "function" one would fulfill for the public good at his own expense. Thus, the liturgy is not something one receives, but rather what one *gives*.

At the same time, as suggested earlier, *liturgy* means "the work of prayer." So the Liturgy is *work*: it is a work that we do together in concert with the Holy Spirit. Consequently, we must expend some effort in order to participate actively and meaningfully. The Liturgy is the *work of prayer*: let us begin by listening carefully, in order to learn to pray properly. It is the *work of the people*; thus, it necessitates a community. At

Introduction

least one other Orthodox Christian must be actively present with the bishop or priest in the praying of the Liturgy in order for it to take place. There are no private liturgies. The Liturgy needs a community for its proper celebration. With the apostolic minister presiding at the Holy Table, at least one other person, and with an offering of bread and wine, the Liturgy may proceed.

The Liturgy is a mosaic of Holy Scripture and prayer, all interwoven into an organic whole. Many people have attempted to enumerate how many scriptural quotations and biblical allusions are contained in the Liturgy. Such exercises are profitable, yet it is difficult to arrive at an exact accounting, since almost every word of the Liturgy is deeply scriptural in tone and content, one phrase running into and even overlapping another. By praying and, over time, memorizing the Divine Liturgy, one learns to pray and even memorize a great deal of the Bible. It has been said that while many Christians study the Bible, we Orthodox pray the Bible.

The Organization of the Divine Liturgy

The Three Basic Parts of the Liturgy

THE PROSKOMIDI

THE FIRST OF THE THREE PARTS of the Divine Liturgy is called the *Proskomidi*, or Preparation. The Proskomidi is completed by the priest in the altar, either before the start of the preceding service (Orthros or the Hours) or during it. This is the only portion of the Divine Liturgy that is served by the clergy without the vocal participation of the laity.

After the priest says some introductory prayers (having said earlier, on his own, the pre-Communion prayers mentioned in Appendix A, "Personal Preparation for Holy Communion"), he enters the Holy Altar and dons his vestments with the specific vesting prayers (mostly citations of select psalm verses) for each article. He then washes his hands. The act of washing the hands is not merely for cleanliness. There is an inscription above the entrance of the ancient Church of Holy Wisdom in Constantinople, a Greek-language palindrome,[4] that means, "Wash your sins, not just your face." By this act of ceremonial washing, the priest demonstrates his rejection of all sin, any grudges, and all impurity. Let each of us faithful draw near to church with the same spirit.

Once vested, the priest does nothing in his own name, but rather all "in the Name of the One who sent him." No bishop or priest possesses the ministry on his own merit; he provides the hands and voice for Christ Himself. The vestments are indicative of the divine, changeless, and life-bestowing grace of the one priesthood of Jesus Christ, who is "He who offereth and He who is offered."

Now the vested clergy (priest along with deacon) are ready to begin the Proskomidi. This preparatory service takes place on a table located to one side in the holiest part of the church building, called the altar or sanctuary. This side table is called the *prothesis*.

The offering that makes this Proskomidi possible,

---

4 NIΨONANOMHMATAMHMONANOΨIN. It reads the same backward and forward in Greek. The author has since noted its use at the Monastery of the Life-Giving Spring, on the *phiale* in front of the church (Dunlap, California).

The Organization of the Divine Liturgy

called *prosphora*, consists of a few[5] loaves of specially prepared bread for each Liturgy that will be celebrated. Ideally, the laity provide the prosphora. It is a great honor and a holy work to bake bread and provide wine for the Divine Liturgy. The bread must have no other ingredients than what the Church prescribes: water, flour, salt, and yeast. No oil or other additive may be used, not even on the baking pans. The prosphora must be well baked after careful preparation. Yeasted bread is always used, since the bread rises and "lives." We never use unleavened bread.

The prosphora loaves are presented beforehand to the clergy in the church and prepared for the Liturgy in this service of Proskomidi. Each of the prosphora loaves provides one element of cut bread to be placed on the special liturgical plate called the *diskos*. Each portion is cut out with exacting detail, all accompanied by specific prayers and exclamations.

From one loaf is cut the "Lamb" marked with the monogram of Christ (IC XC), along with another Greek word (NI KA), in a fourfold pattern, each quarter of which has two letters. The four letters together mean "Jesus Christ conquers." The Lamb

---

[5] Classically five in number, but there is also a custom of providing a single loaf, on which all five cuttings are stamped in miniature.

itself will become the Body of Christ for Holy Communion.

A second loaf yields a triangular portion symbolizing the Mother of God: "At Thy right hand stood the queen" (Ps. 44:10). Then from a third loaf are cut nine small particles symbolizing the ranks of saints and/or angels. The names of many great saints are read as these are cut and placed on the diskos.

After these cuttings have been taken from these first three loaves (or the portions from the one composite loaf), the chalice is prepared. Wine and a small amount of water are now poured together into the chalice, the liturgical cup. The wine must be pure red grape wine (not blush, but dark), naturally sweet, and not fortified. This will become the very Blood of Christ in the Eucharist. The mingling of the wine and the water in the chalice shows that Our Lord on the Cross shed both blood and water to accomplish our salvation, as the Gospel reports: "One of the soldiers pierced His side with a spear, and immediately blood and water came out" (John 19:34). Now that the chalice has been prepared, a small temporary cover is placed over it while the commemorations are taken from the last two loaves.

Finally, the fourth and fifth loaves yield particles for the Orthodox faithful living and dead, respectively. The priest keeps a book of commemorations in which he records the names of many persons for whom he prays: his faithful parishioners, family members, other Orthodox Christians, and others for whom prayer has been requested. Note that the particles for both the living and the dead are assembled together on the diskos. We are in communion with our beloved departed; the Church does not forget those who have died in the faith. The person who bakes the prosphora (him- or herself necessarily an Orthodox Christian) customarily includes a slip of paper on which is written the names of those living and departed for whom prayers are desired.

After all is completely set in order, the diskos and chalice are covered with small veils. Later on, after the Liturgy of the Word, they will be carried in a procession to transfer them from the prothesis table to the Holy Table, the larger table in the center of the altar where the Eucharist will be celebrated.

Now that the diskos is populated with the various particles, we see in a microcosm the whole Church of the living and the departed in one body compact, with Our Lord, "the Lamb of God who taketh away the sin of the world," in the center. The diskos with the Lamb and particles and the chalice with the wine and water within are now both covered with veils, and over both a large cloth is placed, called the *aer*. In front of the prothesis with the diskos and chalice fully prepared and vested, incense is offered with a special prayer of oblation.

This preparatory portion of the Liturgy ends with a general censing of the whole church nave, where the laity stand—usually at about the time the choirs are concluding Orthros (or the Hours). The altar servers gather the remnants of the loaves and cut them up into bite-sized pieces to be served to the communicants to provide for thorough consumption of the precious Gifts, as well as again after the dismissal of the Liturgy to those who were not prepared to receive Holy Communion. These pieces are called *antidoron*, "(a consolation) instead of the Holy Gifts."

THE LITURGY OF THE WORD

The public portion of the Divine Liturgy begins with the Liturgy of the Word. Now we begin the common prayer called the *synaxis*, or the "assembly" of the Christian community. St. Paul admonishes all, "not forsaking the assembly . . . as *is* the manner of some" (Heb. 10:25). From this point on, the community of the faithful joins with the presiding minister—the bishop or his delegate, the priest—in celebrating the Liturgy as a whole. The chief assistant to the presid-

The Organization of the Divine Liturgy

ing minister is also a clergyman, the deacon. One or more altar servers, all of whom are vested for that service, usually assist in the altar as well.

The Liturgy of the Word is made up of "psalms and hymns and spiritual songs" (Eph. 5:19) and has as its climax the reading of selections from the Apostle (the Book of the Acts or one of the apostolic epistles) and the Gospel. In the primitive Church, the Bible was the Sacred Scriptures of Israel, the Old Testament. The congregation would listen to the readings from the Scriptures, then circulate the apostolic letters and read "the memoirs" (St. Justin the Philosopher, early second century), which are called the Gospels. Now we reserve Old Testament reading for festal and Lenten Vespers, and we devote the Scripture readings of the Divine Liturgy to the two most important kinds of lessons from the Bible: the Apostle and, greatest of all, the Gospel itself.

After the Gospel reading, the homily or sermon is delivered.[6] The preacher bears the important task of interpreting to our own situation the sacred words we have just heard. This is the time for the preacher not to promote his own opinions, but rather to bring

---

6 In some parishes, the homily is given at the end of the service, just before the dismissal (although this practice is not considered ideal).

the holy Word of God to bear on our lives so that we become accountable to obey it: "But be doers of the word, and not hearers only, deceiving yourselves" (James 1:22).

We can also characterize this portion of the Liturgy as "of the catechumens" (an ancient nickname), because this was the portion of the Liturgy in which the Holy Scriptures were read and the homily preached. Those preparing for Holy Baptism, the catechumens, were required to be present so they could learn the teaching of Christ in preparation for their baptism. At the end of this portion of the Liturgy, the catechumens were dismissed.

Throughout the Liturgy of the Word, all of us—the faithful, the catechumens, and those inquiring into the Faith (in ancient times called *auditores*, "hearers")—are presented with holy teaching accessible to the ear. "Faith *comes* by hearing, and hearing by the Word of God" (Rom. 10:17). This being said, keep in mind that all the senses are employed in liturgical action in order to raise the whole person to God: we see icons and processions, we smell burning incense and beeswax candles, we touch the icons and make the sign of the cross, we taste Holy Communion. God speaks to us through all of our senses, and beyond—to the heart.

The Organization of the Divine Liturgy

THE LITURGY OF THE EUCHARIST

After the dismissal of the catechumens (a practice not always observed in all churches), the faithful continue in prayer toward the high point at which the Mystical Sacrifice will be accomplished. This is the final and culminating portion of the Divine Liturgy.

After a series of litanies in which petitions are offered "for all men ... lifting up holy hands" (1 Tim. 2:1, 8), the solemn offering is made. The bread and wine, prepared earlier, now are taken up in procession (called the Great Entrance) and placed on the Holy Table. With great compunction of heart, the faithful join with the celebrant in remembering the saving life, death, and Resurrection of the Lord, including His command to "take, eat" and to "drink." The celebrant calls down the Holy Spirit upon the synaxis of the faithful and upon the Gifts, remembering the saints and all the faithful. The faithful then join in saying the Lord's Prayer together, and with other prayers all make ready the chamber of the heart and body to receive Holy Communion. After the Precious Gifts are distributed to all, with concluding prayers the dismissal is said and all "depart in peace."

So now that we have surveyed the entire Liturgy, we can move on to look at each part in more detail, asking ourselves always this question: How can I participate?

Entry into the Church

PREPARATION AND ENTRY, INWARD AND OUTWARD

In general, prayerful participation in the Divine Liturgy calls for preparation well before coming to the church temple. It is important to find silence and inner composure before coming to church. Consider the long period of silence in which righteous Job immersed himself before speaking about God (see Job 2:13). Further, the Lord Himself observed silence with His disciples before ascending Mount Tabor, when He was seen by them transfigured in glory. Practically speaking, in our busy world, we should at least keep the evening before the Liturgy in quietness and prayer. Then, in the morning, holding our hearts in prayerfulness and not speaking too much beforehand, we depart to church.

Some people have the custom of arriving at church and immediately going to an area to talk to others. Of course it is wonderful to greet one another, but we put the Lord last in this way. First, let us greet the Lord Himself. Then, after the Liturgy, we can and ought to greet one another. So we immediately go into the church nave and greet the Lord in quiet prayer and veneration. If others greet you, politely smile and keep your greeting soft and short. In silence we best prepare our hearts and minds to be single, to be focused, to receive the Lord.

THE THREE SECTIONS OF THE CHURCH

We must say something about the shape of the Orthodox church temple, so that we may enter it properly and know our place within it.

The Narthex

We enter the narthex from the noisy world outside and there prepare for prayer: taking off our coats, turning off our cell phones, taking a breath and warming up or cooling down as needed. Then, after leaving an offering of money in support of the parish and of the good causes sponsored by the parish, we take tapers (candles) and any printed aids available for the divine services. If icons are provided in the narthex, we can venerate these before entering the nave.

The Nave

We stand before the doors (or colonnade) leading from the narthex into the central area of the church, the nave. This word comes from the Latin *navis*, or "ship." We may think of the nave as the "hold" of Christ's Church, in which His precious cargo, men, women, and children, are carried into the harbor of the kingdom of heaven.

Opening the door (or passing through the colonnade), we make a *metania* (bow) and reverently enter the nave. In the nave, we may light candles and place them by the icons. The lighting of a candle as an act of prayer provides a concrete way to beseech the Lord in behalf of others, both the living and the departed. It is not proper to venerate the icons or light tapers during the procession of the Gospel Entrance, the reading of the Apostle or Gospel, the homily, the procession of the Great Entrance, or during the *Anaphora* (the central prayer of the Eucharist).

If we are present when Orthros (or the Hours) concludes, we notice the Holy Doors being opened just prior to the beginning of the Divine Liturgy.[7]

The Altar (Bema, or Sanctuary)
The Holy Doors both separate and conjoin the nave with the holy altar or the *bema*, the "high place,"

---

7 The Holy Doors are opened before the Great Doxology is chanted. In churches that say the Hours, the Doors will be opened just before the Liturgy begins.

The Organization of the Divine Liturgy

where the Holy Table is centered. Here, only the clergy and their assistants enter in order to fulfill their work.

We all face east; we are properly *oriented*, both literally and metaphorically.

Now let us take a closer look at the Liturgy. With a copy of the Divine Liturgy in our hands,[8] let us walk through it, seeking to understand what we are doing. The emphasis here falls on a practical way of understanding that will yield more active and more attentive participation in the movement of the Liturgy as prayer. We begin with the priest's opening exclamation of the Divine Liturgy as a whole, "Blessed is the Kingdom of the Father and of the Son and of the Holy Spirit." Let us attend!

---

8 The text of the Divine Liturgy as given in any Orthodox prayer book will serve.

INDICATIONS OF BODILY ACTION
AND POSTURE IN THIS COMMENTARY

CAPITAL LETTERS
indicate the action or posture conforms to
universal Orthodox practice.

lowercase letters
indicate the action or posture is generally
accepted but is not required.

Italicized letters
indicate the action or posture remains
unchanged from one heading to the next

3

The Divine Liturgy in Detail

The Liturgy of the Word (Enarxis and Readings)

THE ENARXIS (BEGINNING)
OF THE DIVINE LITURGY

(ALL STAND AND MAKE THE SIGN OF THE CROSS)

+ "Blessed is the Kingdom..."

THE OPENING OF THE HOLY DOORS[9] symbolizes the act of God drawing near to us in this world. God takes the initiative in coming into our darkened space. Remember, in the ancient Israelite temple, the curtain of the holy place was permanently closed. No one could ever open it. The Evangelist St. Matthew reports, however, that when the Lord died on the Cross, "the veil of the temple was torn in two from

---

9 The exact timing of the opening and closing of the Holy Doors and/or the curtain behind them varies among jurisdictions and from parish to parish.

top to bottom" (Matt. 27:51). Christ destroyed that which divides us from God. The way to God is now open to us, and He invites us to draw near.

So the first words of the common Liturgy now sound forth with a great voice from the priest: "Blessed is the Kingdom of the Father and of the Son and of the Holy Spirit, now and ever and unto ages of ages." The Liturgy begins with the exclamation of God's awesome Kingdom breaking into human affairs. "Blessed is," not "Blessed be." It is truly an exclamation, not a wish. Now He enters our world again, right now, through us.

We begin the Liturgy in a standing position. "Bless the Lord . . . ye that stand in the house of the Lord" (Polyeleos, Ps. 134:1–2). Standing is the basic bodily posture of prayer. Even the repentant tax collector stood "afar off" in prayer (Luke 18:13). And Jesus said that when we "stand praying" (Mark 11:25), we ought to forgive everyone. Christian worshippers stand for prayer and sit for listening (we may sit during the apostolic reading and the sermon, but not for the Gospel reading). In this booklet, we note when sitting is permissible.[10]

---

10 In the Russian tradition, standing is preferred throughout the Liturgy (except during the homily) for those who have the strength. Thus worshipers in that tradition should ignore

The Divine Liturgy in Detail

At the opening exclamation, "Blessed is the kingdom," all the people respond with the one-word prayer, "Amen." This simple prayer is very powerful. The laity should learn to pray it with great intention. It basically means that the one saying the *Amen* takes up the prayer or exclamation that has just been uttered as if it were his or her very own. St. Jerome of Bethlehem (early fifth century) said the Divine Liturgy as it was celebrated in the Church of the Holy Sepulcher in Jerusalem, right at the Empty Tomb itself, was so robust that the laity said "Amen" with the force of a thunderclap. Reach for this prayer and use it often. Consider it your responsibility as a layperson to say the *Amen* properly, in order to mark your active prayer in concert with the presiding minister and the rest of the community.

THE LITANY OF PEACE

(one may be seated)

Now the deacon utters the Litany of Peace, also known as the Great Litany, a chain of petitions in response to which all the people sing the simple and deep prayer, "Lord, have mercy." The deacon does

---

indications to be seated.

this standing on the *solea*, the area in front of the Holy Doors, which in some churches is raised up a bit from the rest of the nave. St. Sophronius, Patriarch of Jerusalem (seventh century), says that spiritually the *solea* represents "the river of fire separating the sinners from the righteous" (Dan. 7:10). Later, the faithful will approach the *solea* to receive Holy Communion, thus crossing this symbolic barrier.

Perhaps you have heard of the Jesus Prayer ("Lord Jesus Christ, Son of God, have mercy on me, a sinner"). When we pray "Lord, have mercy," this is a short version of the Jesus Prayer. God grants mercy; He "sends rain on the just and on the unjust" (Matt. 5:45). It is we who lack mercy. When we pray this prayer with constancy and faith, as the Church teaches us to do, we are purifying our own hearts, which are crowded with the desires and concerns of this world. St. John Chrysostom teaches us in the pre-Communion prayers, "The house of our soul is desolate and fallen." So the Church, in leading us to say this beautiful prayer quite often in the Liturgy, urges us to discover the rich mercy of God. God already abounds in mercy toward us and is eager to enter our defiled bodies and grant us His rich mercy: "And the Lord passed before [Moses] and proclaimed, 'The Lord, the LORD God, merciful and gracious, longsuffering and abounding in goodness and truth'" (Ex. 34:6).

The choir or chanter(s) leads the laity in the singing of "Lord, have mercy" (and in many other liturgical prayers and hymns). The people ought to join in unison with the choir and pray as they sing. Choirs exist in the churches in order to lift up all of the laity in their prayers and hymnody to God. There is a beautiful synergy of worship between clergy, choir, and people. The laity benefit by becoming caught up in this triad. The choirs are leaders for the laity; they know the services well and give the laity a firm foundation for their worship.

The Litany of Peace is a school of prayer in itself. Notice the progression of petitions and reflect upon the course of prayer as it unfolds from a simple plea for peace to an encompassing of the whole world and everyone in it in the loving and merciful embrace of the Lord. Notice the beginning: first, the proper atmosphere of true prayer is peace. Without peace, we cannot pray at all: "In peace, let us pray to the Lord." Then, with peace, we pray for the highest kind of peace: "the peace from above." Jesus said, "Peace I leave with you. My peace I give to you; not as the world gives, do I give unto you" (John 14:27). Only then, having this "peace which passes understanding," do we pray for "the peace of the whole world."

Sometimes our priorities are askew. The Great Litany helps us organize our prayer so that first things come first. We pray for the most important persons first, our spiritual fathers who care for our souls (to gain immortality by grace), then for the civil authorities who govern our temporal lives. After that, we pray for all humanity, in its various states and conditions, and lastly, for ourselves, with a final prayer from the deacon, "Help us, save us," to which we add "Lord, have mercy."

The deacon, like an angel, intones these petitions in a resonant voice. If there is no deacon, the litanies (and some other diaconal parts) are assumed by the priest. Happy are the parishes where the diaconate is active, since they see a beautiful "ministering angel" holding aloft his *orarion* (the long, fluttering stole that directs our attention), carrying the prayers of the people from the nave to the altar and the Holy Gospel from the altar to the nave. The deacon is the ordained minister who "serves" in the fundamental sense rooted in the Gospel itself. Since the deacon moves so often between altar and solea, we call the north and south doors (on either side of the Holy Doors) through which he passes, the "deacon's doors."

The Divine Liturgy in Detail

THE ANTIPHONS

(one may remain seated)

After the Great Litany, we begin to chant a series of *antiphons*; these are short repeated refrains interspersed with verses from the Psalter, the great prayer book of the Church.

The psalms are the verses of the Old Testament most often quoted in the writings of the New Testament. St. Athanasius the Great teaches us, "The psalms prophesy Christ . . . and reflect the entire psychological make-up of man." The refrains on the psalm verses help us to ascend from the affairs of this world to a vibrant realization of the presence of God in our midst.

In the first antiphon, we implore the Savior, Jesus Christ, to save us through the prayers of His Mother: "Through the intercessions of the Theotokos, O Savior, save us." Here, our Orthodox understanding of the role of the Mother of God (*Theotokos*, "God-bearer") is clarified. She is, above all, our great intercessor. She is not an apostle who teaches; rather, she is a mother who entreats for us.

In the second antiphon, we continue to implore the Son of God to save us: "O Son of God, who art risen from the dead, save us who sing to thee. Alleluia." In the third antiphon, we employ the *apolytikion* (hymn of the day) as the refrain. On Sundays, these refrains always mention the Resurrection, and on feast days the apolytikion mentions the theme of the feast. As a unit, the antiphons prepare us for what is ahead, especially the reading of Holy Scripture.

We are still in the early stage of the Liturgy. There are some variations during this portion of the Liturgy, depending on the parish and the practice of each diocese. In some churches, the monastic practice of chanting the "typical psalms" (Psalms 102 and 145) is followed by the chanting of the Beatitudes (Matthew 5) with interspersed hymnody taken from the Orthros service just past. And in other churches, the antiphons are chanted.

Each of the first two antiphons, or two typical psalms, is completed by a little litany, a very short series of petitions, with a concluding blessing from the priest. We use the little litanies so often that the question is frequently posed, "Why do Orthodox services constantly repeat so much material?" Indeed, each little litany begins, "Again and again, let us pray to the Lord." The words "again and again" emphasize repetition.

The wisdom of the Church Fathers is evident

here. When we leave church after the Liturgy, these holy prayers resound within our minds and into our hearts, offering us an artesian well of spiritual refreshment. So the litanies are a prayer drill to teach us how to say quietly at all times, "Lord, have mercy."

During the Great Litany and the little litanies said by the deacon, the priest simultaneously offers specific prayers (often said quietly) that dedicate the Liturgy to God and underscore the divine promises that make the Liturgy possible, including the word of Our Lord, "Where two or three are gathered together in My name, I am there in the midst of them" (Matt. 18:20).

THE LITTLE, OR GOSPEL, ENTRANCE

(ALL STAND)

During the third antiphon (or toward the end of the singing of the Beatitudes), the deacon carries the Gospel book aloft in a liturgical procession, preceded by candle-bearers and the processional cross.[11] Following him comes the presiding priest, who will give the blessing to make the Entrance.[12] The deacon cries

---

11 In the Greek and Russian traditions, the cross is not always carried.
12 It is from later history that the names "Little" and "Great

out the first of several utterances to come: "Wisdom!" This cry always precedes an important utterance or action and exhorts us to pay special attention at the deepest level of our being. Let us now be aware of Christ, the "Wisdom of God" (see Prov. 8), along with the ministering angels in our midst.

The deacon continues, "Stand aright!" At this point, any of the faithful who have been sitting arise to join all who have been standing, ready to make a bow as the Entrance is made. Now the great recognition of Christ in our midst occurs as the entrance hymn is intoned by the clergy and choirs: "O come let us worship and fall down before Christ." All make a metania (bow from the waist) to honor the manifestation of Christ in His public ministry, which this Entrance symbolizes. The Gospel book is the image of Jesus Christ, the living and abiding Word of the Father. "In the beginning was the Word, and the Word was with God, and the Word was God" (John 1:1).

When the bishop presides at the Liturgy, only at this point does he enter the altar to begin actively celebrating there. Up to this point, there is no difference

---

Entrance" derive. This Gospel entrance is the Entrance *par excellence*, since it initiates the Liturgy of the Word. The later, Great Entrance is the ceremony of the "transfer" (the older word) of the Bread and Wine from the Prothesis to the Holy Table.

The Divine Liturgy in Detail

between a Liturgy presided over by a bishop and one presided over by a priest. But now, when the bishop enters the altar, we see the fullest display of our apostolic heritage. When the priest serves alone, it is not easy to see the apostolic nature of the Church. But when the bishop presides, a living apostle is before us. All this shows us that the beginning part, the *enarxis*, has passed, and now the Liturgy of the Word enters its most important stage.

THE HYMNODY AFTER THE ENTRANCE: TROPARIA, KONTAKIA, AND TRISAGION

(ALL REMAIN STANDING)

After the Entrance, the choirs lead the faithful in chanting the *troparia*. Orthodox hymnody is made up of a great many short hymns that are easy for the faithful to learn. These are the troparia, and those applicable to the given day are now chanted. There can be as few as one and as many as four (when there are combined feasts). All the faithful should learn to sing their own parish's patronal or titular festal troparion. This is usually chanted at every Divine Liturgy except on great feasts. In this patronal hymn resides the spiritual ethos of the saint or feast after which one's home parish is named.

After the sequence of troparia, the clergy or choir will sing the appointed seasonal *kontakion*.[13] Some of these kontakia are sung so often they are easily memorized. When all the faithful sing, they show their active ownership of the Liturgy and so fulfill their God-given vocation to be "a holy people, a royal priesthood."

Now, after an exhortation to pray, the priest exclaims the holiness of God, and all sing majestically the simple and profound *Trisagion*, "the Thrice-holy": "Holy God, Holy Mighty, Holy Immortal: have mercy on us."[14] The Trisagion is chanted several times. We may make a metania and sign of the cross at each rendition. The faithful now emulate the heavenly, angelic chorus Isaiah the prophet heard when he beheld the Lord in His holy temple: "Holy, holy, holy *is* the Lord of hosts" (Is. 6:3). The attribute "holy" cannot be described adequately with human analogies. Basically, "holy" means "separated unto and thus belonging to God." Only God is holy in and of Him-

---

13 In some traditions, only one kontakion is chanted; in others, there can be more.

14 On certain feasts of the Lord, in place of the Trisagion, we sing either the baptismal hymn, "As many of you as were baptized into Christ have put on Christ. Alleluia," or that of the Cross, "Before Thy cross, we bow down in worship, O Master, and we glorify Thy holy resurrection."

self, utterly holy, and He makes holy all who come to Him: "You shall be holy, for I the LORD your God *am* holy" (Lev. 19:2), and "Pursue . . . holiness, without which no one will see the Lord" (Heb. 12:14).

When the bishop celebrates the Liturgy, the Trisagion is sung elaborately, with a special psalm verse used as a prayer and episcopal blessing given by the bishop three times interspersed throughout the hymn: "Lord, Lord, look down from heaven and behold and visit this vine, and perfect that which Thy right hand hath planted" (Ps. 79:15). The bishop holds in his left hand the *dikerion*, a two-branched candelabrum symbolizing the two natures of Christ (His divinity and His humanity), and in his right, the *trikerion*, a three-branched candelabrum symbolizing the three Hypostases[15] of the Holy Trinity: Father, Son, and Holy Spirit. Thus, in the bishop's hands the central dogmas of the Church are shown as living and abiding truths that give our lives spiritual order and meaning.

Dogmas in Orthodoxy are not dead concepts inscribed on paper; rather, they are living truths that correct our waywardness and heal our lives from the disorder of sin and corrupting passions. The

---

15 The theologically accurate word, in place of which we often say "Persons."

imprinting of such central dogmas as the two natures of Christ and the Trinity of God provides a therapy bringing the faithful into a truly God-shaped way of life. Dogmas disclose life to the believer, not just information.

THE READINGS: APOSTLE AND GOSPEL
General remarks
While the Trisagion is being completed, the tonsured reader, or someone capable of assuming this task, approaches the solea with the Apostle (the book with the New Testament readings from the Acts and the Epistles) and prepares to intone the reading appointed for the day.

Newcomers to an Orthodox service of worship notice immediately that the manner of speaking in the church differs from what one finds in our everyday world. Ours is a special kind of language, elevated and classical. Even our way of merely reading differs: the reader intones, or reads out in a melodic fashion, plainly but piously, confidently yet with humility. There are many old manuscripts showing the scriptural texts marked with special signs that indicate exactly how the text was to be chanted. St. John of San Francisco said that chanting and reading in a proper church fashion delivers the message contained much more deeply into the souls of those listening than mere recitation. Because readers require specialized training, the Church includes readers among the minor clergy, along with subdeacons.

Prokeimenon and Apostle

(all are seated)[16]

After taking our seats for the reading, sitting erect with uncrossed legs, we focus our attention on the holy apostolic words.

The choir (or reader) intones the *prokeimenon*, "a text before (another) text." This consists of a psalm-verse refrain along with a verse from the same psalm. Originally, the whole psalm was chanted, using the one-verse refrain, repeatedly sung by the people. Now the prokeimenon is heavily abbreviated, usually with just one or two verses. The Sunday prokeimena can be sung according to one of the eight liturgical modes or melodies, or sometimes they are merely read. The prokeimenon prepares us for the lesson from the Apostle. It is designed to adjust our hearing spiritually to take in the profound message from the Apostle reading.

---

16 In the Russian tradition, only the clergy sit during the prokeimenon and Apostle.

COME, LET US WORSHIP

After the prokeimenon, we hear the apostolic reading. The Orthodox liturgical calendar specifies a reading for each day of the week, beginning from the previous Pascha (Easter) and continuing throughout the year. There is frequently another apostolic reading for the saint or commemoration assigned to most calendar dates. We select one of those to be read out, according to specific rules.[17] This is called a *lectionary*. We always hear from one of the epistles of St. Paul on any Sunday.

Everything is done in the Church "decently and in order," with no one, not even the priest, exercising his own will apart from the common and Holy Tradition. The lectionary gives us an orderly presentation that all Orthodox churches share. In the prokeimenon, we receive prophecy; in the Apostle, instruction; and then in the Gospel, the Word Himself.

Alleluiarion and Gospel

(ALL STAND)

Now, as the choir begins to sing the *alleluiarion*, or the triple alleluia,[18] and the deacon or priest is censing

---

17 In some traditions, both readings are performed.
18 Like the prokeimenon, the alleluiarion also used to be a complete psalm, both in the East and the West (where it is called

—62—

The Divine Liturgy in Detail

about the altar, we are ascending even higher. The smoke of the incense honors the Lord and indicates the upcoming climax of this section of the Liturgy. We cense before the climax of the Liturgy of the Word—namely, at the Gospel—just as we cense before the climax of the Liturgy of the Eucharist—namely, at the placing of the Gifts upon the Holy Table.

The Apostle warmed our heart for Christ. Now Christ our God will directly speak His life-bestowing Word (see John 6:63) through the Holy Gospel. The Gospel is chanted by the deacon or priest, accompanied by altar lamps. Even before the Gospel is read, we engage in the first substantive liturgical dialogue with the celebrating clergy. The deacon encourages spiritual readiness: "Wisdom! Let us attend," and the bishop (or the priest) grants the blessing of Jesus Christ: "Peace be to all."

This is what Jesus said when He appeared to His disciples and apostles after the Resurrection. They were locked up in their chamber "for fear." Now Christ gives us the Peace, as we are locked up in the chamber of our heart and beset with many fears. How

---

the Gradual), with triple alleluia as the refrain. Now it is limited to the triple alleluia alone. But in some traditions, the enunciation of two verses from the relevant psalm accompanies the triple alleluia.

often Our Lord says, "Do not fear; peace be to all!"

The Gospel book remains front and center on the Holy Table, always the prominent position. The book itself can be ornate and costly, its binding and covers made of fine metal, enameled or set with stones.[19] When this majestic Book is opened, we stand attentively. Before and after the Gospel reading, we sign ourselves with the cross while saying, "Glory to Thee, O Lord, glory to Thee."

The sign of the cross is the most profound act of prayer the limbs of our body are capable of. At important liturgical moments like this, but also in or out of the church temple, by day or by night, during any endeavor and facing any temptation, we can make the sign of the cross and immediately be refreshed with a vibrant spiritual realization of Christ's holy presence.

THE HOMILY, OR SERMON

(ALL ARE SEATED)

---

[19] I have read that Iveron Monastery (on Mount Athos) makes use of a Gospel book that is so large, with a weight of some 32 kg, that it takes two deacons to carry it in procession. A similar large Gospel book was also employed during a recent Antiochian Liturgy, presided over by H. B. Patriarch John X, on Sunday, June 29, 2014.

The Divine Liturgy in Detail

When the bishop is absent, the authorized preacher is the priest or deacon, and the permitted themes for the sermon are drawn from the appointed scripture lessons and the saint's or festal commemoration of the day. Sometimes the bishop gives special instruction concerning what is read or said from the pulpit. The homily or sermon[20] provides the hearers with a clearer understanding of the sacred words they have heard and the meaning of the specific teachings conveyed by the day's commemoration.

For Orthodox Christians, the sermon, although far too often undervalued and even in some places neglected, remains a vital element in the whole of Liturgy. We must keep in mind, however, that the sermon plays a much less prominent role in Orthodox Christian worship than it does in non-Orthodox assemblies. The reason for this is simple. Our purpose for gathering in the church is not merely to hear what the priest has to teach us, but rather to bring our "sacrifice of praise" to the Lord.

The role of the laity during the preaching of the sermon is to listen carefully and to take to heart those elements from the homily that strike home. Our homilies are usually quite short; frequently the Orthodox

---

20 Both words, from the Greek and Latin languages respectively, simply mean "a talk."

homily is no more than fifteen minutes long. Even small children can learn to listen with care. Elder Zacharias of Essex says that the core of a good sermon is "one simple thought, deeply expounded."

The Liturgy of the Eucharist

(ALL STAND)

THE TRANSITIONAL STAGE WITH PRAYERS[21]
Four specific litanies are said before the transfer of the bread and wine from the prothesis to the Holy Table, which begins the Eucharist. The first of these litanies is called the *fervent ektenia*. We pray for all in this ektenia (extended litany) of fervent supplication, (*fervent* because now we say "Lord, have mercy" three times after each petition). Unlike the earlier litany of peace, we may even pray specifically for persons by name, both living and departed. Any of the faithful may supply to the deacon before the beginning of the Divine Liturgy written names of specific Orthodox Christians for mention in the fervent ektenia. We mention aloud the names only of Orthodox Christian faithful in this ektenia. Each believer can

---

21 In some traditions, these prayers are sometimes shortened or entirely omitted.

pray for his or her non-Orthodox loved ones personally when lighting a candle when he or she first enters the church.

The second of these litanies is called the *litany of the catechumens*. This petition for the catechumens makes mention of all the elements necessary for life as a Christian: "Instruction in the word of truth, revelation of the gospel of righteousness, union with the holy catholic and apostolic Church." This petition reminds the faithful of their foundation as Christians. The catechumens are then dismissed, marking the formal end of the Liturgy of the Word.

In the primitive Church, the catechumens were ushered out of the *synaxis* (assembly of the faithful), and the doors were secured. In some monastic churches, even until the present, non-Orthodox are ushered out of the nave at this point in the Liturgy. In the early era of the Church, the catechumenate was in a vibrant state of development. Adults came to Christ directly from paganism and, as a result, they needed exorcism, thorough instruction in prayer, knowledge of Holy Scripture, and instruction in the practical way of Christian life. The new converts had to rid themselves of many un- and even anti-Christian habits of thought, speech, and action.

After Christianity was officially recognized and

even promoted by the Roman Empire, all the citizens were Christians. The need for adult catechesis greatly decreased, and only babies needed baptism. But now, in our day and age, in which the Christian spiritual and ethical conscience in society at large has greatly declined, the adult catechumenate is increasingly being reinstated. For many years this litany in behalf of the catechumens was omitted, but now it is increasingly needful as more converts ignorant of the basics of Christianity are finding their way home to Orthodoxy. Also, the faithful themselves can hear in these words a dismissal of all evil thoughts and an expulsion of every distraction.

Finally, two short litanies, each called "litany of the faithful," provide closure to this prayerful transition. The quiet prayers said by the priest while the deacon intones the short petitions deal with the priest's own need for inner purification and readiness to lead the Eucharist.

All is now ready for the transfer of the Holy Gifts to begin the eucharistic offering. Now the faithful attend to the solemn acts that lie before them: the bringing of the gifts of bread and wine to the Holy Table, and the Eucharist itself.

The Divine Liturgy in Detail

THE CHERUBIC HYMN AND THE TRANSFER OF THE GIFTS

(ALL REMAIN STANDING)

The choirs now chant the Cherubic Hymn very slowly with great ornamentation and beauty. This hymn is an expression of our emulation of the holy angels who accompany the Lord in glory. The image depicted in the hymn is drawn from the ancient Roman military ritual of acclaiming a new emperor. The soldiers would hoist the newly chosen leader on a shield, and all would point their spears straight up and utter their oath of loyalty. So we say in the cherubic hymn, "the King of all, who comes invisibly upborne (literally, 'carried with raised spears') by the orders of angels." Thus, we present ourselves in an angelic state, bearing the Lord Himself as we utter the thrice-holy hymn (which is about to be sung in its oldest form, in the *anaphora*, discussed below).

Most importantly, we now put aside the cares of daily life. These cares are not necessarily bad or sinful, but merely mundane and transitory. St. John Chrysostom says, "The soul that has not learned to despise the petty concerns of everyday life will not be able to marvel at the things of heaven." We ought, then, to leave them for our later attention, as we place our minds and hearts fully on the holy *anaphora,* or *oblation.* God does not want us to shirk our daily and mundane responsibilities; however, He does want us to put them in proper perspective. Right now, all else is secondary to the Eucharist.

While the choirs are singing the Cherubic Hymn, the priest says a prayer in a quiet voice beseeching God for the grace to serve Him without offense in the coming Eucharist. These quiet prayers of the priest can be read by the faithful in their prayer books. In this prayer, we learn that Christ Himself is both the chief Celebrant and the Offering: "for Thou Thyself art He who offereth and is offered."

There is a special censing, showing the solemnity of the moment, just as there was for the climax of the earlier Liturgy of the Word, before the Gospel. After this censing, during which the celebrating priest prays Psalm 50, the most profound expression of repentance in the entire Bible, he makes a reverence toward the people. This is the expression of reconciliation and forgiveness we must extend to each other if we are to "bring our gift to the altar" in a worthy manner. We ought never to participate in the Liturgy, as clergy or laity, if we bear ill will against another human being.

The Divine Liturgy in Detail

The procession leading to the Great Entrance divides the Cherubic Hymn in the middle. Whereas in the Little Entrance, the Gospel book is borne, symbolizing Christ's appearance in His public ministry, so now in this Great Entrance, the *diskos* and *chalice* are borne, symbolizing Christ's willing self-sacrifice in His Holy Passion (suffering), death, and burial for our salvation. The deacon bears the diskos and the priest the chalice, and they are preceded by candle-bearers and the cross.[22]

In antiquity, there was a separate building or side chapel where the bread and wine were prepared and lodged. As this part of the Liturgy approached, the deacons would take up the gifts and bring them in a procession to the bishop, who awaited them in front of the altar. Now we keep the gifts on the prothesis table, where they were prepared in the Proskomidi, earlier. The procession from the prothesis to the Holy Table marks the formal beginning of the anaphora or holy oblation (offering).

In some traditions, there is a pious custom during the procession through the nave for the faithful to briefly touch the priest's *phelonion* (the outer cape) as he passes, in a tactile way participating in the

---

[22] The processional cross is not used in the Russian tradition.

procession itself. Consider how in this procession the priest is the image of Christ, "who, in the press of the crowd, was touched by the woman with the issue of blood." She was healed by this act of faith. So this practice is commendable, as long as it consists of a brief touch and never a grasping of the vestment (small children will need help with this).

In the procession, it has become customary to make special commemoration for Orthodox Christians, including the chief hierarch of the local church, the diocesan bishop, and the civil authorities. Formerly, no commemorations were said here, but only the words "All of us, the Lord God remember in His kingdom." In many churches the litanies that precede the entrance are omitted, so it has become customary to mention names of Orthodox Christians at this point.

In most churches we name the chief hierarch of the church and the civil authority. It is always important to bear in mind that the Orthodox Catholic and Apostolic Church does not subscribe to any political party or specific political system. We do, however, pray for the welfare of the civil authority, recognizing that all authority comes from God (see Rom. 13:1).

The procession now reaches its climax as the priest and deacon enter the Holy Doors and place

The Divine Liturgy in Detail

the bread and wine on the Holy Table. While they enter, the choirs conclude the Cherubic Hymn. The gifts are placed upon the previously unfolded *antiminsion* (Greek, from the Latin, "in place of the [bishop's] Table"; in English, commonly abbreviated to *antimins*). This is a special cloth bearing the icon of the bodily repose of our Lord Jesus Christ after He was taken down from the Cross: "In the grave with the body, but in hades with the soul as God; in paradise with the thief, and on the throne with the Father and the Spirit wast Thou, O Christ, filling all things, Thyself uncircumscribed."

This cloth is signed by the metropolitan archbishop of the local church. The antimins represents the license from the hierarch for the Divine Liturgy to be served at the specific church where it is placed. No Liturgy can take place without an antimins. Every antimins has a precious relic of a saint sewn within it. In the early Church, the Christians celebrated the Liturgy over the graves containing the relics of the holy martyrs. Later, when churches were built, the Holy Table was invested with holy relics at its consecration. We do this up to the present day.

The use of the antimins developed to allow for the Liturgy to be performed in an unconsecrated location. The presence of a relic is important because it shows the connection of the earthly Church with the heavenly Church, the imperfect conjoined with the perfect. One can think of the antimins as a portable altar. It has become mandatory that an antimins be used everywhere, even on consecrated altars. The antimins is always protected, when folded up, by a red cloth called the *eiliton*.

AUGMENTED LITANY

(one may be seated)

Once the gifts have been placed on the Holy Table, a prayer and a litany are offered that sum up all our desires for salvation in every state of life. We "complete our prayer unto the Lord" by appealing to God for the fulfillment of our needs, culminating in the greatest need of all, "that we may have a good defense before the fearful judgment seat (*bema*) of Christ." This petition is important, since the name of the very place where the gifts have been placed is the *bema*, "the judgment seat," one of the many names for the altar. We realize that the judgment is not only in the future, but even right now! Are we ready to meet the Lord? Will we be found worthy to partake of Him?

The Divine Liturgy in Detail

THE PEACE BEFORE THE EUCHARIST

(ALL STAND)

With the sober reality before us that we stand before the judgment seat of the King of all, once again we hear the holy words to calm our hearts, "Peace be to all!" We heard these words before the Gospel; now we hear them before the confession of faith. Our inner disposition is peace; without inner peace, we are mouthing empty words.

SYMBOL OF FAITH (THE CREED)

(ALL REMAIN STANDING)

"Let us love one another, that with one mind we may confess . . ." How can we confess the holy dogmas of our faith while we harbor hatred and unforgiveness in our hearts? The Church's Liturgy examines us carefully in this regard. So the exchange of the "kiss of peace" is our guarantee of Christian charity and reconciliation, each person with his neighbor. "Thou shalt love the Lord thy God . . . and thy neighbor as thyself." Each rank of clergy and the laity, as necessary, then exchange a fraternal greeting before we confess our faith together. St. Paul tells us, "faith work[s] through love" (Gal. 5:6) and "greet one another with a holy kiss" (2 Cor. 13:12).

(ALL SAY OR SING THE CREED TOGETHER)

Before the Creed is said or sung, we hear the diaconal exclamation, "The doors! The doors!" This is a call to secure the doors between the nave and the narthex, in order that no unworthy person, heretic, persecutor, or unbaptized be allowed in. This was practiced by the Church in ancient times. We still say these words in order to instill seriousness in the act of confessing our faith. Every Christian should say these words aloud together with the community.

The Symbol of Faith, or the Creed
(credo, *Latin, "I believe"*):

> I believe in one God, Father Almighty, Creator of heaven and earth, and of all things, visible and invisible. And in one Lord Jesus Christ, the Only-begotten Son of God, begotten of the Father before all ages; Light of Light, true God of true God, begotten not created, of one essence with the Father; through whom all things were made; who, for us men and for our salvation, came down from the heavens and was incarnate of the Holy Spirit and the Virgin

Mary, and became man. He was crucified for us under Pontius Pilate and suffered and was buried; and He arose on the third day according to the Scriptures; and He ascended into the heavens and is seated at the right hand of the Father; and He shall come again with glory to judge the living and the dead; whose kingdom shall have no end. And in the Holy Spirit, the Lord, the Creator of life, who proceedeth from the Father, who with the Father and the Son together is worshipped and glorified, who spake through the Prophets. In One, Holy, Catholic, and Apostolic Church. I acknowledge one Baptism for the forgiveness of sins. I look for the resurrection of the dead, and the life of the age to come. Amen.

Our sponsors at our baptism made this confession for us, and each believer repeats it in every Liturgy. It consists of specifically composed words that were authorized by the First Ecumenical Council held in the city of Nicaea in AD 325, added to by the Second Ecumenical Council held in Constantinople in AD 381, and sealed with divine authority by the council's decree at the Third Ecumenical Council held in Ephesus in AD 431. Holy men labored long and hard to put into words the very bedrock of our faith. Every element is key to our understanding of who God is, what His purpose is for His creation, and the Way in which we each enter that salvation.

Jesus said, "I am the Way, the Truth and the Life." Imagine a compass heading for a large ship sailing the Pacific Ocean. A mere one-degree error in the compass heading would yield a massive error in sailing by the time the ocean was crossed. The ship's pilot would miss his port by hundreds of miles. Thus, we carefully preserve "the faith which was once for all delivered to the saints" (Jude 3). Every statement of the creed is essential to our Orthodoxy ("right-believing"). The words of the creed are said in the first person, proclaiming that by this statement of our personal will we unite ourselves with Christ's Body—His Church, past, present, and future.

In many churches, during the recitation of each of the twelve articles of the Creed, the church bell is struck once. This striking of the bell underscores the seriousness of our confession. The Creed is truly the flag of the Church.

As the recitation continues with the voices of every worshipping believer, the priest lifts up and waves the *aer* (the covering cloth) over the diskos and chalice, thus revealing the bread and wine. This is the first time they are visible. At the words "and He ascended into heaven," the priest folds up the *aer* and resumes waving it in a circular motion over the gifts.

Such actions as this waving or fluttering of the *aer* are amenable to a great many interpretations of a fine spiritual nature. For example, many see in this a depiction of the hovering of the Holy Spirit, who is about to descend upon the gifts. "And the Spirit of God was hovering over the face of the waters" (Gen. 1:2). From the beginning, many liturgical actions arose from very practical purposes, such as to keep any flying insects from alighting upon the prepared Holy Gifts. Unlike those who see only exterior meaning to things, we Orthodox see both: the waving of the *aer* keeps off flies as well as symbolizing the earthquake that occurred at Christ's Resurrection or the descent of the Holy Spirit at Pentecost.

THE ANAPHORA

(ALL REMAIN STANDING)

The eucharistic dialogue

The climax of the Divine Liturgy now takes place. The holy *anaphora*, the oblation or "offering up (to God)," now begins. A special interchange serves to awaken and employ the highest human sensitivity—

the *noetic* or spiritual ability of the soul. After the call to attentiveness, the deacon says, "that we may offer the holy anaphora in peace," and the faithful add to this a further description of the oblation, thus defining it: "A mercy of peace, a sacrifice of praise." The most acceptable sacrifice to God amounts to "the weightier *matters* of the law: justice and mercy and faith" (Matt. 23:23). "What does the Lord require of you but to do justly, to love mercy, and to walk humbly with your God?" (Micah 6:8).

Before the prayer of the anaphora is uttered, the priest gives the apostolic blessing. This comes from the earliest times of the Church's life: "The Grace of our Lord Jesus Christ, the love of God the Father, and the communion of the Holy Spirit be with you all" (2 Cor. 13:14, and at the end of many of the other epistles).

(ALL INCLINE HEADS AT THE APOSTOLIC BLESSING)

With this blessing, all is in order for the liturgical act. Apostolic orders and blessing have been given; it remains to fulfill them. The faithful have already "laid aside all earthly cares"; now they are exhorted to an even higher, noetic awareness: "Let us lift up our hearts!" The wording suggests a specific action here—not just mental attention, but something much more profound—spiritual attentiveness: "Up (with) the hearts!" "We have them toward the Lord."[23] All join together now for the eucharistic prayer, "Let us give thanks unto the Lord." In response to this, the laity urge the priest to begin the anaphora proper by singing these initial words: "It is meet and right."

Anaphora proper

(ALL STAND, WITH GREAT ATTENTIVENESS)

The anaphora is the whole of the eucharistic prayer, the highpoint of the Liturgy, and is a mighty embodiment of the whole of the apostolic tradition. In it we hear all about "the wonderful works of God" (Acts 2:11).

As mentioned at the beginning, there are various "liturgies" in use in the Orthodox Church: most commonly, those of St. Basil and of St. John Chrysostom. Others exist as well but are rarely used today. Each of these liturgies receives its name from the saint who composed the anaphora in it. In the beginning, the apostles and their successors prayed and celebrated the Eucharist "according to their ability" (Martyr

---

23 This is a very literal translation of the original Greek, to underscore the point.

Justin the Philosopher, *First Apology*, 67, c. AD 150). As the faith spread, there was an increasing need to write down this holy eucharistic anaphora, especially when local bishops began to ordain presbyters (priests) to serve in their absence. Since they could not be present at every Liturgy, the written anaphoras came into being as we now have them.

The anaphora falls into three distinct sections, each of which is marked by a special hymn sung by the people. The initial expression of thanks to God for His mighty acts is completed with the singing of the thrice-holy hymn, directly using the words of the angelic hosts themselves as they chant to the Holy Trinity: "Holy, holy, holy, Lord God of *sabaoth* (a Hebrew word that means 'armies [of angels]')" (Is. 6:3).

The middle of the anaphora, the second section, stresses the manifestation of the love of God by the offering of His Only-begotten Son. "For God so loved the world, that He gave His only begotten Son, that whoever believes in Him should not perish but have everlasting life" (John 3:16); these words are quoted by the priest in the anaphora. The culmination of this section is the rehearsal of the very words of our Lord Himself, uttered by the celebrating priest as though

Christ were physically present: "Take, eat, this is My Body.... Drink of this, all of you. This is My Blood."

After these holy words, which provide the very substance for the whole of the Liturgy, the priest (or deacon) elevates both the diskos and the chalice, holding them in a crosswise fashion. With this action, the anaphora reaches the highest point of human ability in reaching toward God. This is our offering—the simple basics of life, through which the Life of the world will come to us. "Wine maketh glad the heart of man . . . and bread strengtheneth man's heart" (Ps. 103:16–17).

With the elevation, the priest intones solemnly, "Thine own, of Thine own, we offer unto Thee, in behalf of all and for all." Together, clergy and laity voluntarily offer back to God, who gave it, the whole of creation ("Thine own"). And with a special purpose—for the salvation and reconciliation of the whole of creation ("in behalf of all and for all"). This is the ministry of Jesus Christ in miniature; this is the ministry of the Church in depth—to bring all back to God, voluntarily, in the freedom of love.

Immediately, the choir adds a sung response to the words the priest has just uttered: "We hymn Thee, we bless Thee, we give thanks to Thee, O Lord, and we pray to Thee, O our God." This is meant as a completion of the priest's words. Among many other things, this should emphasize that the Liturgy is accomplished by the whole synaxis (assembly) of the laity, not just by the priest alone.

Offering and Epiklesis

(ALL MAKE A BOW [or inclination] AT THE EPIKLESIS)

At once, God answers the elevation by His action. The priest invokes the Holy Spirit (*epiklesis*, "invocation") "upon us and upon these gifts," thus rendering the bread to be the Body of Christ and the contents of the cup to be the Blood of Christ, "changing them by Thy Holy Spirit." We speak of metabolism in the human body as it processes material or physical energy; now the priest mentions a special kind of metabolism ("changing," from the Greek word *metabalon*) in which the Divine Energy infuses the material gifts offered. Our reception of these Gifts will be a meal, but now a unique one, for we will, by faithfully partaking of the Gifts, become communicants in the divine nature.

Unlike the medieval Western Scholastics of old (with their theology of total transformation or "transubstantiation") or the Protestants (who deny transfiguring grace to this mystery, seeing it simply as symbolic), we have no need to explain this great, dual-natured mystery: we have bread, it is the Body; we have wine, it is the Blood. Our understanding gives us the key that holds all together, "holding the mystery of the faith with a pure conscience" (1 Tim. 3:9): we confess Christ as having two natures, divine and human, one person, "without confusion, without change, without division, without separation."[24]

To summarize, the sacred exchange takes place: the worshipping community, represented by the presiding bishop or priest, offers its all, embodied in the bread and wine, "Thine own of Thine own." In response, God receives this offering and "places His own Life in the Gifts, 'the Holy for the holy'" (Elder Zacharias of Essex).

Commemorations (Diptychs)

(ALL REMAIN STANDING)

Once the epiklesis is completed, we enter the third section of the anaphora, in which we commemorate the whole Catholic Orthodox Church. We begin with the departed and greatest members of the Church: the Mother of God, then the apostles and the saints,

---

[24] From the Definition of Chalcedon (AD 451).

mentioning especially those saints we are commemorating on that day, and then by name the faithful departed (especially those newly deceased). Parishioners may notify the priest of departed ones to be remembered by writing their names on a slip of paper and giving it to him ahead of time.

The choir begins singing the *megalynarion* (magnification hymn) to the Theotokos, as she justly receives prime attention. During this hymn, the priest says all the commemorations, and the deacon stands beside the Holy Table, reading out the diptychs (a record of names of living and dead who are to be commemorated). We see ourselves standing by the very Altar of God, with no difference between heaven and earth: "Behold, the tabernacle of God *is* with men" (Rev. 21:3).

The commemorations continue with the first of importance among the living: the hierarch and/or bishop who preside over the parish. We receive our hierarchical authorities not as worldly princes or strong men, but rather as fathers in Christ. In this spirit, they nourish us with apostolic teaching and authority and become the visible, personal, and concrete principle of catholic unity in the Church: "Wherever the bishop is, there are the people all gathered together" (St. Ignatius of Antioch). The commemorations are only complete once every class of Christian has been mentioned, including both monastics and laypeople. This is especially emphasized in the manner in which both genders are noted in the original Greek, literally "and of all men and all women."

We conclude the anaphora in the name of the Holy Trinity; "Thine all-honorable and majestic Name, of the Father and of the Son and of the Holy Spirit." The anaphora, however, is not complete until the whole congregation asserts the "amen." When St. Jerome referred to the *amen* as a thunder clap, he was referring to this *amen*.

We have celebrated the Eucharist, we have given thanks. "The Christ is in our midst! He is and ever shall be!"

THE COMMUNION IN THE HOLY GIFTS

Now that the anaphora is complete, the synaxis prepares for Holy Communion. This preparation consists of a movement toward the common recitation of the Lord's Prayer, the bowing of heads (inclination) toward the Lord in reverence, and the invitation to commune in the form of an elevation of the now consecrated Body. After this, during the slow and solemn chanting of the communion hymn, the priest completes the preparation for Communion by the *fraction* ("breaking of the bread," Acts 2:42) of the Lamb and its placement on the four compass points of the diskos. This is followed by the commingling or mixing of the part of the Lamb marked *IC* (Greek shorthand for "Jesus") with the consecrated wine in the chalice, and then adding the blessed *zeon*, or hot water. Now the clergy commune by taking a part of the Lamb that is marked *XC* (Greek shorthand for "Christ") and then drinking from the cup, the Blood of Christ. Afterward, they prepare the remainder of the Holy Gifts for the Communion of the laity. Let us examine all of this in order.

Preparatory prayers for Holy Communion

(after the priestly blessing, one may be seated)

The priest blesses the faithful, after which there is a litany in anticipation of the Lord's Prayer. This litany emphasizes the importance of the prayer we are about to utter. It is the only litany that leads up to a common prayer said by all. It is usually greatly abbreviated, except when a new deacon has just been ordained. He is given this entire litany as his first to intone.

The Divine Liturgy in Detail

The Lord's Prayer

(ALL STAND AND SAY OR SING THE PRAYER ALOUD)

This pre-Communion prayer is the prayer given to us, exactly word for word, by the God-man Himself, our Lord Jesus Christ. Among the many wonderful things we are taught in the Lord's Prayer, Jesus instructed us to say, "Give us this day our daily bread." This is truly a sacramental Element, not merely bread from the marketplace. The express meaning of this petition in the original language is "give us today the bread which is more-than-daily," or "give us our super-essential bread" (as the ancient Latin translation says). Thus, our Lord taught us to yearn for the eucharistic meal, through which we would receive the Life that never ends. "Do not labor for the food which perishes, but for the food which endures to everlasting life. . . . I am the living bread which came down from heaven. . . . Most assuredly, I say to you, unless you eat the flesh of the Son of Man, and drink His blood, you have no life in you" (John 6:27, 51, 53). In fact, we are taught to pray at least "three times a day" (*Didache of the Twelve Apostles,* second century) the Lord's Prayer, which, in essence, is deeply liturgical and eucharistic.

After the bestowal of peace, there is a prayer of inclination, of "bowed heads."

(ALL STAND WITH BOWED HEADS)

When we hear the admonition to bow the head, this is an invitation both literally to bow the head by bending the neck and also to observe deep silence while the prayer is prayed in our behalf. In the Old Testament, many times the prophets rebuked rebellious Israel. The prophets called them "stiff-necked"; the Israelites rendered themselves incapable of receiving a blessing, because they could not bow the head, they could not humble themselves. It is so important to bow, to bend, to lower oneself. Only then can we receive a blessing. "Therefore humble yourselves under the mighty hand of God, that He may exalt you in due time" (1 Peter 5:6).

The Elevation, the Fraction, and the Mingling
After the priest makes three *metanias*, he reverently takes up the consecrated Lamb to present the formal invitation to Holy Communion. This is four words in Greek, *ta aghia tis aghiis*, which means literally, "the Holies for the holy!" At its very foundation, the word *holy* means simply "belonging to God," as we discussed above. When we say God is holy, it means

that God is completely *other*; that is, there is no part of creation, animate or inanimate, that is part of Him. He is without beginning; nothing in Him was made. He is and always has been. Therefore everything created is outside of God.

However, in His love for the creature, He imparts holiness. This is to say that He makes it *his*. That which is holy becomes pure, set apart, dedicated. The holy cannot now be put to any other use, "for the Lord, whose name *is* Jealous, *is* a jealous God" (Ex. 34:14). He desires that which becomes His to continue to "flourish in the fatherly adoption" (Sunday Orthros). So here, these four words in Greek say so much more than we hear in English. We might render them something like this: "The gifts now consecrated and thus belonging to God are fitting for those persons who are consecrated and thus belonging to God."

How can we include ourselves in this condition? In answer to this, the choir leads the synaxis in the beautiful response, "(Only) One is holy . . . Jesus Christ, to the glory of God the Father. Amen!" So we become holy by our participation in Jesus, the only Holy One of Israel. This is the key, then, to preparedness for Holy Communion: Am I a partaker in Christ, or am I dishonoring Him by my unworthy way of life? "If you love Me, keep My commandments" (John 14:15).

Jesus receives all who draw near with repentance and forgiveness. This is our great comfort. Every Orthodox Christian ought rightly to seek absolution for sins committed, along with soul-saving penance (not punishment, but rather a therapy for the healing of the soul), on a regular basis. When sins are forgiven through the agency of the priest (by virtue of his apostolic orders), the penitent has the baptismal robe, "the garment of light," renewed and is a worthy partaker. So Christian *ascesis* (effort) is essential to preparedness to commune in the sacred Mysteries.

Holy Communion of the Clergy and the Laity

*(ALL REMAIN STANDING AND SAY
THE PRE-COMMUNION PRAYER TOGETHER)*[25]

In order to prepare ourselves most assuredly, we all join together to say the last of the Pre-Communion Service, the prayer of St. John Chrysostom: "I believe, O Lord, and I confess . . ." This prayer contains the fundamental ingredient for worthy Communion, repentant hope: "I will confess Thee: Remember me, O Lord, in Thy kingdom!" Every Orthodox Chris-

---

[25] In some traditions, this prayer is said immediately before the communion of the laity, and sometimes by the priest alone.

tian ought to memorize by word and meaning the holy sentiments of this prayer. In it, we carry all our Christian hope and love.

Usually during this prayer, the priest accomplishes the fraction of the Lamb. The Lamb is divided into four equal portions (along the cuts that were scored in the bread at the Proskomidi or service of preparation), and one is set at each of the four compass points on the diskos, with the commemoration particles in the middle. Three of the four fundamental manual acts have now been completed: the taking up (the Great Entrance), the giving thanks (the anaphora, or Eucharist), and the breaking of the bread (the fraction). There remains only the distribution (Holy Communion). These four actions are specifically mentioned in the scriptural accounts and are mystically revealed in the account of our Lord's feeding of the five thousand (see Matt. 15:36).

The priest places the "Jesus" portion into the chalice with the following words: "The union of the holy Body and precious Blood of our Lord Jesus Christ, and the fullness of the Holy Spirit." This means the accomplishment of the complete chalice for Holy Communion is the work of the Holy Spirit. We commune with God, not by some ethereal magic or some law of necessity, but rather by the radically free agency of God the Holy Spirit.

When in the Liturgy does the bread and wine become the Body and Blood of Christ? This is an important question for many readers. We recognize the power of God in the Liturgy to be both mystical and personal, not magical. Therefore, we cannot point to any precise time when the bread and wine become the Body and Blood of Christ. This is a sacred family meal. Once it has begun, we do not interrupt it.[26] The whole of the Liturgy is an experience of apostolic and catholic fullness. It is Christ Himself re-presenting His once-for-all sacrifice as the One who is both Priest and Victim. This is accomplished by the Holy Spirit. The commingling of Body and Blood is sealed with the addition of zeon, or boiling hot water, to the chalice to symbolize the outpouring of the Holy Spirit: "the fervor (*zesis*) of faith, full of the Holy Spirit."

Holy Communion: Distribution

(*ALL REMAIN STANDING, BEFORE AND DURING RECEPTION OF HOLY COMMUNION.*

---

26 If a serious interruption occurs in the Divine Liturgy before the Great Entrance, the priest may stop the Liturgy. If, however, this interruption occurs after the bread and wine have been placed on the Holy Table, the priest is duty-bound to complete the Liturgy through the Communion.

The Divine Liturgy in Detail

After all have received Communion, one may be seated)

The bishop, priests, and deacons all receive Holy Communion in the altar. All this is accomplished before the Holy Gifts are brought out to the faithful, who commune on the solea, the area directly in front of the Holy Doors. Jesus distributed the bread to the disciples, and then they, in turn, distributed it to the multitudes.

As an indication of what is to come, the deacon cries out, "With fear of God, and faith and love, draw near!" Here are our prerequisites. Do we have due reverence, "fear of God"? "The fear of the Lord is the beginning of knowledge" (Prov. 1:7). Do we believe in Him with Orthodox faith and love Him in accordance with His commandments? If so, we are ready.

(ALL FORM A COMMUNION LINE[27]
AND APPROACH THE CHALICE)

Before the Creed is said, we hear the diaconal exclamation "The doors! The doors!" This is a call to secure the doors between the nave and the narthex in order that no unworthy person, heretic, persecutor, or unbaptized person be allowed in. This was prac-

---

27 Each parish has its own preferred order for forming the line. Some begin with the children, while others simply go from front to back of the nave.

ticed by the Church in ancient times.

After reverently approaching with forearms crossed over the heart (if this is your local practice), we receive the Mysteries. At the moment of taking his or her stand before the priest, the communicant says, "The servant of God, *Baptismal Name*" or simply states his or her name (whichever the priest prefers). We always commune with the name we received at Holy Baptism, whether it is our given name in common use or not. The priest responds, "The servant (handmaid) of God (*Name*) partakes of the precious and most holy Body and Blood of our Lord and God and Savior, Jesus Christ, for the remission of sins and for eternal life."

Directly after receiving the Precious Gifts in the mouth, wipe your lips on the *kalyma* (napkin) if necessary,[28] then make a small step backward away from the chalice. Only then turn aside to take a piece of the blessed bread offered for the purpose of effecting a complete consumption of the small fragments of the precious Gifts that may still be in the mouth. Do not make a sign of the cross before the chalice now, after communing, as this poses a risk of upsetting the chalice.

---

28 It is the custom in some churches to kiss the chalice after partaking of Communion.

The Divine Liturgy in Detail

Later on, after the dismissal, blessed bread will be offered to those who could not partake of Holy Communion (for whatever reason). This final offering of bread is called *antidoron* ("in place of the Gifts") and provides a kind of consolation for the non-communicants. Strictly speaking, those who just received Holy Communion should not take this antidoron, but rather should stay behind and read the post-Communion prayers of thanksgiving (see below for more).

POST-COMMUNION

(ALL STAND)

After Holy Communion, the priest gives a blessing and, on most days, the choir sings the post-Communion hymn of Pentecost: "We have seen the true Light, we have received the heavenly Spirit; we have found the true Faith, worshipping the undivided Trinity, for He hath saved us."[29] This is a recap of all the faithful have experienced in the Liturgy: Christ revealed as Light, heard through His life-giving Word, and accepted in Holy Communion. If

---

29 During Pascha we chant "Christ is risen" here; and at Great Feasts, the special hymn of the feast is chanted at this point.

people ask, we can say that "He hath saved us." More Orthodox Christians ought to be aware of their spiritual life and confident when declaring the mercy of God to others, based on the experience of divine grace that comes through the Liturgy.

We must say something here about the poor habit of some in leaving the church at this point in time. After receiving Holy Communion, we should stay in the nave until the priest says the final dismissal, which brings a formal conclusion to the Liturgy.[30] It is good liturgical manners to honor the Lord by keeping our heart and mind fixed upon Him during the final prayers. We do not leave the dinner table until our divine Host excuses us.

During the singing of the post-Communion hymn, the priest prepares to transfer the unconsumed Holy Gifts back to the prothesis (side table in the altar). As a part of this process, he removes all the remaining particles of bread on the discos and places them into the chalice. This act is accompanied by the words "By Thy precious Blood, O Lord, wash away the sins of Thy servants here commemorated, through the intercessions of all Thy saints." This simple petition sum-

---

30 If one has a responsibility for activities in the life of the church that take place after the Liturgy (church school, agape meal, etc.), he or she is blessed to leave the Liturgy earlier.

marizes our Orthodox understanding of the role of the saints in heaven. Chiefly, they intercede for us, urging on through their heavenly encouragement all of us who struggle in this life. They are a "cloud of witnesses" (Heb. 12:1) who stand with us, inciting us to virtue.

After the chalice is covered and all is put in order, the priest raises the chalice toward the west with the words "Now and ever, and unto ages of ages!" This stresses the promise of our Lord to His disciples, "Lo, I am with you always, even unto the end of the age" (Matt. 28:20, the last words of that Gospel). With this encouragement, we respond to that promise by a petition to the Lord to be established in the sanctification, the holiness, imparted by Holy Communion: "Let our mouths be filled with Thy praise, O Lord" (Ps. 71:8). What was an event, we now desire to become a way of life. That simple yet profound psalm verse ends with the statement of the goal: "that we may meditate upon Thy righteousness." This is the priority of the spiritual life in Christ, for He Himself urged us to "seek first the kingdom of God and His righteousness" (Matt. 6:33).

A short thanksgiving litany is now said. This prompts the faithful who have communed to give proper thanks to the Lord. Remember the account of the healing of the ten lepers. Only one came back and rendered thanks to Jesus. We should not find ourselves numbered among the "nine who did not return to give thanks."

Many parishes now have the blessed custom of reading the entire service of prayers of thanksgiving after Holy Communion, once the dismissal from the Liturgy has been accomplished. Unless some great necessity interrupts, all those who communed should remain in the church temple for these prayers, whether reading quietly from one's prayer book while others are still communing, or attending to them being read afterward (if it is the parish custom). Otherwise, the communicant ought to read these prayers on his own sometime during coming day.

DISMISSAL

(ALL REMAIN STANDING)

"Let us depart in peace!" The Liturgy began in that spirit, "In peace, let us pray to the Lord." And in this same way it concludes "in peace." Now the priest offers a summary prayer, the "prayer behind the amvon," for all people in every state of life. The amvon in ancient church temples was the pulpit, an elevated platform located in the midst of the nave.

The Divine Liturgy in Detail

The priest came out of the Holy Doors, among the people, and stood behind the amvon to pray. This shows the coordinated prayer of the priest with all of the faithful as all are about to depart from the church temple.

The faithful join with the priest in this prayer for all, "give peace to Thy world, and to all of the churches." We say "churches" because we now pray for the specific needs of each local organized sister church, located in a specific place, within the whole of the Universal Church. Orthodoxy is not a theoretical universal concept; it is a specific, tangible organization headed by a chief hierarch in any given locale. The communion of all of these churches amounts to the presence of Christ in the world. In response to the prayer, the faithful sing the threefold declaration of the manifest blessedness of the Name of the Lord, "Blessed be the Name of the Lord, henceforth and forever more."

Now the complete dismissal is said. In the dismissal, the priest always summarizes the commemoration of the day: the Lord Himself, His most holy Mother, and all the saints, naming especially the patron of the parish church and those whom we festally commemorate that day. This leaves us with a warm disposition to continue our inner prayer once we depart. We go forth in order to bring Christ into the world, not to leave Him in the church temple. The final word of the Divine Liturgy is a long form of the Jesus Prayer: "Through the prayers of our holy Fathers, Lord Jesus Christ our God, have mercy on us and save us." To which all respond, "Amen."

The dismissal is complete. The custom of distributing *antidoron*, blessed bread, while the hand-cross is venerated provides the occasion for the reading out of the post-Communion prayers. The deacon consumes the remainder of the Holy Gifts, all the clergy remove their liturgical vestments, and after making three bows, they "depart in peace."

Unfortunately, some have taken up the habit of engaging in small talk in the nave, and even in the altar, while the post-Communion prayers of thanksgiving are said. This disturbs the quietness and prayerfulness that have been cultivated for the last hour and a half. All should reserve any talk for outside the nave once all are gathered together for the customary agape meal, the common meal of the parish. Outside, at the common table, all eat and share their joys and sorrows with love and serenity. We will have much to share one with the other in the love of Christ, who now dwells afresh within us.

The Divine Liturgy in Detail

Concluding Remarks

The Divine Liturgy bestows a profound dignity on the faithful. It also involves a serious and high duty: to reconcile all the world to God. St. Paul said to his spiritual children, "God was in Christ reconciling the world to Himself... and has committed to us the word of reconciliation" (2 Cor. 5:19). So the living Word is now implanted in us who have received Him. It is now up to us to live this and to bring others to Christ through our Christian example and selfless love.

The Divine Liturgy is a work of great beauty. The purity of the simple human voice uncluttered with mechanical instrumentation, the perfume of incense, the soft, warm, and fragrant glow of the waxen tapers, the many-colored icons, vestments, and glitter of liturgical vessels, all raise our whole being in prayer and imbue us with a holy purpose. High and exalted language, in its classical and refined form, rather than common, everyday language—all these characterize the Divine Liturgy. Yet let this not be an outward beauty only, for God "looks upon the heart." Let us match the outward beauty with an inward disposition of repentance, humility, and obedience, lest the word of the prophet indict us: "these people draw near to Me with their mouth, . . . but their heart is far from Me" (Matt. 15:8; see also Is. 29:13).

It is fitting to conclude with the final words uttered by our father among the saints, St. John Chrysostom, son of Antioch and Archbishop of Constantinople, that great pastor, preacher, and liturgist:

Glory to God for all things!

+ + +

Here ends the reading of this study . . .
Now for the living of it!

Appendix A

Personal Preparation for Holy Communion

THE FOLLOWING ELEMENTS of preparation may be considered foundational for approaching to commune in the sacred Mysteries of Christ. Your spiritual father provides the necessary details regarding the frequency of partaking and preparation for Holy Communion in a personally applicable way.

✠ You must examine yourself to be sure you have no ill will, unforgiveness, or rancor toward anyone. "If you bring your gift to the altar, and there remember that your brother has something against you, leave your gift there before the altar, and go your way. First be reconciled to your brother, and then come and offer your gift" (Matt. 5:23–24).

✠ You ought to have recently confessed your sins before your father confessor and received absolution and a blessing to receive Holy

Communion. There are varying expectations among priests regarding this. Talk to your parish priest about the frequency of confession, and how to confess, if this is new to you. The canons of the church require that all Orthodox make confession during Great Lent in preparation for Paschal Communion. However, St. John Chrysostom censures those who prepare only this one time and then go on to live heedlessly once again. We should always be confessing!

✠ Out of respect for the Lord, you should refrain from reception of Holy Communion if you arrive late to the celebration of the Divine Liturgy. The parish priest usually establishes this precise rule; in many parishes, those who would commune need to be present for the hearing of the Holy Gospel in the Liturgy of the Word.

✠ We observe a strict fast from all food and water from the previous evening (no eating or drinking after midnight, for morning Liturgy). In the event of an evening Liturgy, we begin this eucharistic fast from no later than the noon hour (some require fasting throughout the whole day).[31]

---

31 These rules may be relaxed in individual cases if the commu-

Appendices

✠ "May a woman properly enter church at the time of menstruation? And may she receive Communion at these times?" (a question of St. Augustine of Canterbury addressed to St. Gregory the dialogist, pope of Rome, early seventh century). In short, a woman may enter the church and may receive Holy Communion, because the bodily movements do not make a woman unclean. St. Gregory responded to this question with the following: "The workings of nature cannot be considered culpable . . . her condition is beyond her control." St. Gregory adds, "If it was a laudable presumption in the woman who, in her disease, touched our Lord's robe, why may not the same concession be granted to all women who endure the weakness of their nature?" Finally, he concludes, "When women after due consideration do not presume to approach the sacrament of the Body and Blood of the Lord during their courses, they are to be commended. But if they are moved by devout love of this holy Mystery to receive as pious custom suggests, they are not to be discouraged." (Venerable Bede, *History of the English Church and People*, bk. 1, 27.8)

---

nicant's health requires it. This is up to the discretion of the priest.

✠ We say the pre-Communion prayers in three units:

1. Many say the Pre-Communion Canon before bed the night before (designed to be said with Compline; however, it can be said with the usual evening prayers). This prayer takes fifteen minutes.

2. Most will say the pre-Communion service consisting of the trisagion prayers, three psalms, three troparia, and nine pre-Communion prayers, all of which are to be said on the morning of the Liturgy, before coming to church or in church before the Liturgy begins. The entire pre-Communion service takes twenty minutes to read out in full.

3. All will say the tenth pre-Communion prayer, said in the Liturgy just before Holy Communion itself: "I believe, O Lord, and I confess…"

Appendices

In order to receive eternal life into ourselves, let us approach Holy Communion with a pure soul and with burning desire. Let us cross our hands [one upon the other], and receive into them the Body of the Crucified One. And after touching it with our eyes, our lips and our foreheads, let us partake of the divine Coal. Thus the fire of our love will be ignited by the divine Coal, and burn up our sins and illumine our hearts; and through participation in the divine fire, we shall catch on fire and be deified [made Godlike].

HIEROMONK GRIGORIOS,
CITING ST. JOHN OF DAMASCUS, EIGHTH CENTURY

Appendix B

Laymen Entering and Serving in the Holy Altar

The easternmost portion of the church temple is called the Holy Altar or Sanctuary. This area is reserved to the ordained clergy and the men or boys who are given a blessing to assist them in their sacred ministry at the Holy Table. Each priest in his own parish church, following the directives of his bishop, expresses his requirements to those who assist him in somewhat differing ways. The following guidelines may be considered as widely applicable.

✣ No layman enters the altar without a priestly blessing.

✣ Altar servers should dress in a dignified and respectful manner, as directed by the priest. Since both the neck area and the shoes are visible after donning the sticharion, a collared or turtleneck shirt is recommended, with the top collar button fastened. Dark socks and dark polished (or otherwise clean) shoes for the feet. Shirts should have no loud color or imprint that may be visible through the sticharion or distract attention at the collar. The sticharion should properly extend to touch the shoe below the sock line when the server is standing erect.

✣ Anyone who enters the altar approaches the north or south deacon's door, venerates the icon on it, opens the door, and enters, then closes the door (or curtain) behind him noiselessly. In the manner in which the parish priest has instructed him, he reverences toward the Holy Table and then proceeds as follows.

✣ For the Divine Liturgy, the altar server proceeds to the area where the vestments are kept. He folds his sticharion (about this, see further, below) into a unit with the cross on the back facing upward. Bearing the vestment upon his palms, he approaches the priest and says, "Father, bless!" The priest blesses with his hand and then places his hand upon the folded sticharion. The altar server kisses the priest's hand, and then he kisses the cross on the sticharion and withdraws to vest.

Appendices

- ✠ The sticharion, as with any vestment, should never be placed on the floor for folding; this is disrespectful to sacred things. Folding can be accomplished on any table or even in the air, with training.

- ✠ The altar servers are to maintain silence and to keep their eyes upon the priest, in order to be at the ready for any need. The priest should never have to speak to gain the attention of an altar server. We avoid all talking or disruption to the ministry of prayer, which dominates service at the holy Table. Parish priests usually work out sign language or give the altar servers their own marked booklets to follow.

Appendix C

Standing or Sitting in Vespers and Orthros

This book deals with the Divine Liturgy only. However, it seemed logical to provide a note about posture at the other common services in the parish, since these services are increasingly well attended by pious communicants in the Divine Liturgy.

Vespers with an Entrance (always on Saturday evening)

We stand up (if seated) at the following points:

✠ "Blessed is our God" and remain standing through the end of Psalm 103.

✠ "O Lord I have cried" and remain standing until the censing is completed.

✠ "Both now" and remain standing until the

Entrance is concluded and "Gladsome Light" is finished.

✟ At the exclamation, "For Thou art a good God" and remain standing through the prayer of bowed heads. (If the Service of Litia and Artoklasia is to be celebrated, we remain standing throughout it.)

✟ At the diaconal prompt, "Wisdom!" and remain standing through the dismissal from Vespers.

Orthros with a Gospel Reading (always on Sunday morning)

We stand up (if seated) at the following points:

✟ "Blessed is our God" and remain standing through the end of the Six Psalms. Note: During the Six Psalms we do not move about in the nave and do not even make the sign of the cross.

✟ "That we may be accounted worthy to hear the Holy Gospel" and remain standing until the veneration of the Gospel is completed.

✟ "The Theotokos and Mother of the Light" until the censing at the ninth ode is completed.

Appendices

- ✷ "Glory to Thee who hast shown us the light" and remain standing through the opening exclamation of the Divine Liturgy.

These directions are general; check for specific details with your priest and refer to your parish customs for more clarity.

Glossary

The following is an alphabetized listing of specialized vocabulary in common use when speaking of the various elements of the Divine Liturgy. Pronunciation schemes are supplied for certain difficult words. G. = Greek; H. = Hebrew; L. = Latin.

Aer (G., *ah-EAR*) The decorated cloth that covers both *diskos* and *chalice* from the conclusion of the *Proskomidi* until the recitation of the *creed*.

Agape Meal (G., *ah-GAH-pee*, "love") In the early church, the common meal in the midst of which the Eucharist was celebrated. Now, the common meal shared after the Liturgy is completed.

Alleluia (H., *AH-leh-LOO-ee-ah*, or *AH-leh-LOO-yah*, "Praise the Lord") This "spiritual song" is chanted before the Gospel lesson as an expression of spiritual ascent to God. It remains untranslated in all languages, like *amen*.

Alleluiarion G., the triple *Alleluia* sung thrice in three sets, with two intervening psalm verses, which, as a whole, prepares the faithful for the hearing of the holy *Gospel*.

Altar The area of the church temple where the *Holy Table* is located and into which only the clergy enter. Also called the *Bema,* Holy Place, or Sanctuary.

Ambon, or **Amvon** G., either spelling is pronounced *AHM-vohn*. The pulpit located in the middle of the nave in the church temples of antiquity. It has one use now: "the prayer behind the amvon," a general intercession said by the priest on the *solea* before the dismissal from the Liturgy.

Amen H., *AH-MEN*, the chief prayer of the people by which they agree with and confirm the exclamations and extended prayers of the celebrant. The "Amen" is a necessary adjunct in the Liturgy, as it must come from the laity and shows the synergy required of the laity for the Liturgy to be served. It remains untranslated in all languages, like *alleluia*.

Anaphora G., *ah-NAH-pho-ra,* also called (based on the Latin equivalent) *oblation*; the "offering-up," the portion of the Liturgy of the Eucharist which begins with the dialogue and encompasses the whole of the eucharistic prayer. The anaphora comprises the heart of the Liturgy.

Glossary

Antidoron   G., *ahn-DEE-thoh-rohn*, "instead of the Gift," the cut-up remains of the loaves from which the Lamb and other particles were taken in the preparation service. This was formerly handed out at the end of the Liturgy only to those who were not prepared to receive Holy Communion, as a consolation. Today, in most parishes, all receive the antidoron when they venerate the hand-cross held by the priest.

Antiminsion   G., *ah-dee-MIN-see-on,* or simply, **Antimins**. The cloth, bearing the image of the repose of the Lord after the taking down of His Body from the Cross and signed by the diocesan or metropolitan hierarch, which is unfolded upon the *Holy Table* for the celebration of the *Eucharist*. Traditionally, a sacred relic is invested in the antimins, if it is to be used upon an unconsecrated table.

Antiphons   G., so named since they were meant to be chanted by two choirs, back and forth. Any of the three opening bodies of psalmody (or fragments thereof, as is commonplace now) with verses and refrains that serve to prepare the faithful for the solemnities of the Liturgy.

Apolytikion   G., *ah-poh-lee-TEE-kee-on*, "dismissal hymn" (since it is chanted at the end of Vespers and Orthros), a *troparion* that carries the theme of the saint or festivity of the day.

Apostle The first scriptural reading drawn from the Acts of the Apostles or from the Epistles of Paul, James, Peter, John, or Jude. Popularly called the "Epistle"; however, the Acts of the Apostles is not an epistle, therefore the term is not sufficiently inclusive.

Bema G., *VEE-ma*, "high place, judgment seat," a reference to the *altar* as a whole, as we speak of "ascending" to the altar of God.

Beautiful Gate The double doors located in the center of the *iconostasis*, the chief link between the *altar* and the *nave*. These doors, also called the **Holy Doors** or, less accurately, the **Royal Doors**, open to a full view of the *Holy Table* during festal moments in the divine services.

Bishop The chief rank of minister in the Church, a successor to the Apostles. The bishop personifies the whole Church in any given place.

Catechumen G., *CAT-eh-KYOO-men*, "one under instruction," an unbaptized person who is preparing for Holy Baptism.

Chalice The liturgical cup that contains the commingled wine and water for the *Eucharist*. Also referred to by its Greek name, *poterion*, somewhat preferably, since the holy chalice is usually adorned with

Glossary

icon(s), whereas a Western chalice is frequently much simpler in design.

Cherubic Hymn The entrance hymn sung for the *Great Entrance,* so named from the opening words, "Let us who represent the cherubim." There are only two times in the year when an alternative hymn is chanted for the Great Entrance: Holy Thursday and Holy Saturday.

Creed The Symbol of the Faith, "I believe in One God."

Deacon The ordained clergyman who assists the *bishop* (or *priest*) with a specific liturgical role of directing various actions and petitioning in prayers.

Deacon's Doors The north and south doors that pierce the *iconostasis* on either side of the *Beautiful Gate*. The *deacon* frequently passes through the Deacon's Doors to lead the prayer-*litanies* and for other purposes.

Dikerion G., *dee-KEE-ree-on*, the two-branched candelabrum wielded by the *bishop* to depict the two natures of Christ. In his other hand, the bishop also holds the *trikerion* (G. *tree-KEE-ree-on*), the three-branched candelabrum that symbolizes the three Hypostases (Persons) of the Holy Trinity.

Diptychs G., *dip-ticks*, the record of the living and the dead (literally, "two folds" to accommodate the two groups), read out quietly by the deacon during the commemorations in the *anaphora*.

Diskos G., *diskarion*; the liturgical plate (Latin, *paten*) upon which are arranged the *Lamb* and the commemorative particles for the *Eucharist*. We prefer the term *diskos* (or, more accurately, *diskarion*) over *paten*, since the latter possesses no stem but lies flat upon the table.

Doors (Holy) Common name for the *Beautiful Gate*. These open the altar to the nave. Sometimes incorrectly called the Royal Doors (this term, strictly speaking, refers to the great doors at the main entrance of a cathedral leading into the narthex from the outside).

Eiliton, see **Iliton** G., the "corporal," a silken cloth that is used to cover the folded *antiminsion*.

Ektenia G., an "extended" *litany*, or chain of petitions, intoned by the *deacon*, to which the people pray "Lord, have mercy" three times after each petition.

Entrance In the Liturgy, the ending portion of the procession from the nave into the altar through the *Beautiful Gate*. There are two: the *Little Entrance* (with the Gospel Book) and the *Great Entrance* (with the offered bread and wine). The Little Entrance introduces the Liturgy of the Word, and the Great Entrance introduces the Liturgy of

Glossary

the Eucharist.

Eparchy G., *EH-par-hee*, "subsidiary rule," an ecclesiastical province that is subject to a greater province.

Epiklisis G., *eh-PEEK-lee-sis*, "invocation," the solemn act in which the celebrant calls down the Holy Spirit for the *metabolism* of the offered bread and wine to become the Body and Blood of Christ.

Eucharist G., *YOU-kah-rist*, "thanksgiving," the central mystery of the Liturgy culminating in the reception of Holy Communion.

Fraction L., "breaking (of the bread)," the third of the four manual actions of the Eucharist, performed just prior to the distribution of Holy Communion. It is the ancient name for the Eucharist (Acts 2:42), the breaking of the bread.

Gifts, Precious Gifts The consecrated bread and wine, as the Body and Blood of Christ, given in Holy Communion.

Gospel The second and chief scriptural reading taken from one of the four Gospel books of the New Testament. In some cases, a composite Gospel is read, in which selections from more than one of the Gospels are drawn.

Guardian Angel An angel appointed by God to protect

and to give guidance to the faithful. At Holy Baptism, a guardian angel is appointed to accompany the new Christian until repose from life.

Homily G., "a talk," also called *sermon*, in which the Word of God is proclaimed and interpreted from the scriptural passages just read to the pastoral situation at hand.

Iconostasis G., "icon screen," also called the *templon*, which serves to mark the division between the nave and the altar.

Iliton, or **Eiliton** G., *ee-lee-TON*, the red cloth that protects the antimins folded up underneath the Gospel Book.

Jesus Prayer A prayer of varying length, using some or all of these words: "Lord Jesus Christ, Son of God, have mercy upon me, the sinner."

Kontakion G., a seasonal hymn, sung as the last *troparion* after the Entrance and just before the chanting of the *Trisagion Hymn*.

Lamb The central portion of bread (marked with a seal in four quarters, from upper left to lower right, IC XC NI KA for "Jesus Christ conquers"), which is cut out and placed in the center of the *diskos*. The Lamb itself will become the Body of Christ in the *Eucharist*.

Glossary

Lesson L., *lectio*, "Reading." See **Reading**.

Litany A chain of petitions to which the faithful respond with "Lord, have mercy" (once after each petition) or "Grant this, O Lord." There are little, great, and augmented litanies.

Liturgy Properly called the **Divine Liturgy,** the primary act of Christian worship, celebrated by an apostolic minister (the *bishop* or delegated by him to a *priest*) along with a congregation of faithful laity (the *synaxis*).

Lord's Prayer The prayer beginning with the words "Our Father who art in heaven," taught to His disciples by Christ.

Memorial Also called "trisagion for the departed," a service of hymns and prayers for the souls of the faithful who have passed from this life in the hope of the resurrection. The Church appoints memorials on the first, third, ninth, and fortieth days after the date of bodily death, and anniversaries after that. It is customary to offer *kollyva* ("KOH-lee-vah"), a mixture of boiled wheat grains, sweet fruits, almonds, and other ingredients, as a sign of faith in the general resurrection (see John 12).

Mystagogy G., "initiation" into the mystery of our salvation. A patristic name for the Divine Liturgy.

Matins (British, **Mattins**) See Orthros.

Megalynarion   G., *meh-gah-lee-NAH-ree-ohn,* "Magnification hymn" sung to the Mother of God during the commemorations in the *anaphora*. In some places it is followed by another megalynarion sung in commemoration of the saint or feast of the day, while the anaphora is concluded.

Metabolism   The Orthodox reference to the "change" that occurs in the bread and wine during the Divine Liturgy.

Metania   G., *meh-TAH-nee-ah,* "repentance." This may refer to the little metania, a bow from the waist with an outstretched and open right hand to the floor, or to the great metania, a full *prostration*.

Mysteries   G., *mysteria,* always plural in the sense of referring to both the Body and the Blood of Christ in the Eucharist. In the singular, **Mystery**, a sacrament (in which case it is capitalized), and also a way of expressing the dual nature of existence: both spiritual (noetic) and material. The Orthodox Church views all her rituals as mysteriological, i.e., as means of divine grace for the healing of man.

Name Day   The commemoration day of the saint after whom an Orthodox Christian is named at baptism. The Church considers this day to be more important than the anniversary of one's birth, since the observance of the name day in church commends the believer to God in a personally profound way.

Narthex The space in the Orthodox church *temple* through which one passes to enter the *nave*. Baptisms and certain other services are sometimes held in the narthex.

Nave L., "ship," the central place of worship for the Orthodox Christian within the *temple*, viewed in the metaphor of the hold of Noah's ark.

Noetic G., *no-EH-tic*, "mental, spiritual," refers to the human capacity for spiritual knowledge (G., **nous**) in contrast to rational, or discursive, knowledge.

Oblation L., "*anaphora*, offering," used in the opening dialogue of the anaphora, "Let us offer the holy oblation (*anaphora*) in peace."

Orarion G., the deacon's stole, the end of which is elevated at certain times to visually stimulate the people toward more intentionality in prayer.

Orthros Also popularly called *Matins*, the morning prayer service, with hymnody for the given day's commemoration. We prefer the term *Orthros*, as the term *Matins* chiefly evokes the Western (Roman Catholic) order for morning prayer, which differs in several particulars.

Pantocrator G., "ruler of all." The title of Jesus Christ attributed to Him in the Book of Revelation (see chapter 1). Also, the title of the icon of our Lord in which He is depicted enthroned as Ruler of all, or as adorning the top of the interior of the central dome of the church.

Pericope G., "(literary) passage." A scriptural passage (prophecy, apostle, or Gospel) appointed to be read in a service of worship. See *reading*.

Phelonion G., (linguistic metathesis from *phaenolion*, etymologically equivalent to the L. *paenula*) "cloak," the priest's outer vestment symbolizing solemn beauty and joy in liturgical action. This vestment is only worn at festal services (which include every Divine Liturgy) or moments in a given service that call for festal celebration.

Priest G., from its older form, "presbyter" ("elder" or "veteran"). The apostolic minister who serves the Holy *Mysteries* (sacraments) with the *bishop's* authority and who may serve as pastor of a parish community.

Prokeimenon G., *pro-KEE-meh-non*, "pre-text," a psalmic refrain with one or more verses drawn from a given psalm. In the Liturgy, it prepares the people for the reading from the *Apostle*.

Glossary

Proskomide G., *pros-koh-mee-DEE*, "presentation," the service of presenting and preparing the bread and wine for the *Eucharist*. Frequently anglicized as **Proskomidi**.

Prosphora G., *PROS-for-ah*, "offerings," the round loaves of bread prepared for the *Eucharist* by hand-kneading (usually) and stamped with special seals. The Liturgy itself as a whole is also called the Prosphora.

Prostration L., a great *metania*, or full bow, touching the forehead to the floor.

Prothesis G., "setting forth," the table located in the north area of the altar, and often within a cave-like indent, upon which the *Proskomidi* service is performed.

Qurban (Arabic, "offering"). The bread offered from which the Lamb is cut to become the Body of Christ, along with the blessed leftovers. See also *Antidoron* and *Prosphora*.

Reading Also called *lesson*. A selection of Holy Scripture appointed to be read during the Liturgy of the Word. See *Apostle* and *Gospel*.

Relics L., "remains." Fragments of a saint's bodily remains (primary) or of a saint's personal effects, such as clothing, etc., which had contact with his or her body (secondary). The Church has always treated the relics of saints with great respect and views them as a life-giving source of divine grace. The earliest account of a martyrdom outside of the New Testament itself, *The Martyrdom of Polycarp,* mentions the collection of the relics of St. Polycarp. The Seventh Ecumenical Council (eighth century) decreed that relics should adorn every church. Relics are customarily invested in the Holy *Table* when it is consecrated by the bishop at the establishment of a new church. A relic is also sewn into the *antiminsion.* Also, relics are often set forth in the nave for the veneration of the faithful and become a source of great spiritual and bodily healing.

Sacristy L., "area for sacred things," called in Greek, the *diakonikon* (since the deacon maintains this area) or *skevophylakion*, since liturgical vessels (*skevi*) are kept there. It is the area of the altar to the south of the Holy Table where vestments and liturgical items are kept and maintained.

Solea L., the raised area between the nave and the sanctuary where the *litanies* are intoned, the *Apostle* is read, and the faithful receive Holy Communion.

Synaxis G., *SEE-nahk-sis*, "gathering," the assembled faithful people, i.e., the liturgical community as a whole. Also a reference to the specific liturgical synaxis that occurs on the day after a great feast, in which the secondary person(s) of the feast are commemorated, with the name of "the Synaxis of *Name*."

Table, Holy The focus area of Orthodox Christian worship upon which the *Eucharist* is celebrated. The *altar* is not the Table but rather the area of the church where the Holy Table is located.

Temple The church building itself.

Theotokos G., "birth-giver of God," the dogmatic title (decreed by the Third Ecumenical Council) of the Virgin Mary that guarantees against Nestorianism, the heretical view that Jesus and Christ are two separable entities.

Throne-on-high, or **Cathedra** The bishop's throne, located in the apse to the east of the Holy Table. There is provision for this in only some churches, since from the time of the filling in of the templon to become an iconostasis, the bishop sits enthroned in the nave, on the south side.

Transfer G., *metaphora*. The act of moving the prepared Gifts from the *Prothesis* Table to the Holy Table by means of the procession and Great Entrance, just before the *Eucharist*.

Trikerion The three-branched candelabrum wielded by the bishop that symbolizes the three Persons of the Holy Trinity (along with the *dikerion*).

Trisagion Hymn G., "thrice-holy," the hymn sung just before the scriptural lessons, "Holy God, Holy Mighty, Holy Immortal, have mercy on us." On certain great feasts, an alternate is sung.

Troparion G., the generic term for a short hymn for which there are various names depending on the specific use: apolytikion, kontakion, etc.

Vespers L., the evening service of prayer that initiates the new liturgical day.

Vestry The area of the altar used for storing and donning the diaconal and hieratic vestments. See *sacristy*.

Wine Also called (G.) *nama* to distinguish wine for the Liturgy from all other wines: dark red grape, very sweet, and not artificially fortified. The wine is mixed with water in the *proskomide*, and the *zeon* is added to this just before Holy Communion, in the Liturgy.

Zeon G., *ZEH-on*, "hot," boiling water added to (commingling with) the consecrated *wine* in the *chalice* just before Holy Communion. Holy Communion is administered warm, to physically symbolize the divine and dynamic nature it bears as the mystical Body and Blood of Christ.

About the Author

The V. Rev. Fr. Patrick B. O'Grady, B.A., M.Div., is a lifelong pastor and an Orthodox priest. In addition to being active in parish ministry throughout his career, he has assisted the Antiochian Orthodox Archdiocese of North America by providing oversight in liturgics and translation. Fr. Patrick contributed to the *Orthodox Study Bible* (Thomas Nelson, 2008) and has published many articles on liturgical themes. Currently, he is a doctoral candidate and also serves as Chair-Professor of liturgical theology for the Antiochian House of Studies, which he helped to found.

We hope you have enjoyed and benefited from this book. Your financial support makes it possible to continue our nonprofit ministry both in print and online. Because the proceeds from our book sales only partially cover the costs of operating **Ancient Faith Publishing** and **Ancient Faith Radio**, we greatly appreciate the generosity of our readers and listeners. Donations are tax deductible and can be made at **www.ancientfaith.com**.

To view our other publications,
please visit our website: **store.ancientfaith.com**

Bringing you Orthodox Christian music,
readings, prayers, teaching, and podcasts
24 hours a day since 2004 at
www.ancientfaith.com

www.ingramcontent.com/pod-product-compliance
Lightning Source LLC
Chambersburg PA
CBHW030334100526
44592CB00010B/693